THE UNITY WE SEEK

THE UNITY WE SEEK .

A Statement
by
the Roman Catholic/Presbyterian-
Reformed Consultation

Edited by

Bishop Ernest L. Unterkoefler
Dr. Andrew Harsanyi

BTQ
414
.R65
1977

Bx
1789
.P73
R65
1977

PAULIST PRESS
New York/Ramsey/Toronto

172310

Library of Congress
Catalog Card Number: 77-74579

ISBN: 0-8091-2027-5

Published by Paulist Press
Editorial Office: 1865 Broadway, New York, N.Y. 10023
Business Office: 545 Island Road, Ramsey, N.J. 07446

Printed and bound in the
United States of America

Contents

Introduction

History of the Roman Catholic/Presbyterian-Reformed Consultation, 1965-75

After much reflection I have decided to write this history in the first person. My reasoning is that it will better represent the factual situation. This introduction is not an agreed-upon statement but a presentation by one person who must take responsibility for the points of view, the evaluations, and the biases represented here. Only in this way can the rest of the members of the consultation have freedom to criticize or dissent. Secondly, these ten years have been one of the most extraordinary and enriching experiences of my life. It would not be possible for me to disengage that experience from what I write about the history of this consultation. As a French church historian once said: "We all have our prejudices but thanks be to God mine are the right ones."

An exploratory meeting between the representatives of the two traditions took place in Washington, D.C. on July 27, 1965. It was decided to divide the consultation into two sections: a Theological Section and a Worship and Mission Section. This was the only bilateral consultation in the United States between the Roman Catholic Church and other communions to be so structured. In retrospect the division had definite limitations, the primary one being that until the last three years the two sections interacted very little. One result is that this history of the consultation is being written very largely from the standpoint of the Theological Section. However, viewing the work that was done by the Worship and Mission Section, I believe they made a most valuable contribution to the cause of ecumenism, for they pioneered in a number of sectors of ecumenical cooperation that must precede the work of Christian unity.

The first meeting of the newly constituted consultation was May 26-29, 1965, in Philadelphia, Pennsylvania. Two papers were discussed: "The Role of the Holy Spirit in the Church" and a proposal on common worship. At this meeting the two sections met jointly at all the sessions, about twenty-five or more persons around the table. This made discussion unwieldy, often repetitive, and frequently at highly diverse levels of concern. This was particularly true of the theological paper. It had been put together by a small group and largely by phone. This fact, plus the desire to give no offense and establish as much common ground as possible, resulted in the paper's being frequently ambiguous or ambivalent. In addition, as might be expected, an air of tension was present because no one was quite sure how to handle this new experience in a group whose members did not know one another or were, at best, acquaintances. Consequently, the discussions were basically defensive, each one anxious not to betray his or her own tradition. The meeting concluded with fairly general dissatisfaction. Looking at it from this time vantage of ten years, I see it as an absolutely necessary first stage in the learning process of ecumenical dialogue.

Out of this whole experience two decisions were made. First, the two sections in the future would meet separately and have one joint session to report their work to each other. Second, in the Theological Section two papers, one from each tradition, would be presented at meetings. Finally, in order to focus on some of the issues raised in the discussion, and because of its historical connotation, the topic chosen for future dialogue in the Theological Section was Scripture and Tradition.

The second meeting was held May 12-15, 1966, in New York City. The papers presented in the Theological Section were: "Tradition Apostolic and Ecclesiastical" by Martin Anton Schmidt and "Scripture and Tradition: A Roman Catholic View" by John L. McKenzie. For the other section Christopher Kiesling presented a background paper entitled "The Purpose of the Worship and Mission Section." The first two papers have been published in the jointly sponsored *Reconsiderations*.[1]

This second meeting was much more satisfactory. The groupings were smaller and more homogeneous. Moreover, because most of us had already met, it was much easier to search out one another's views and understand them. Thus we began the effort to learn each other's theological style and language. The stance taken was much less defensive and far more concerned with understanding the other's position. This approach was in large measure due to the excellence of the papers and their presenters. Out of the discussion gradually emerged the topic for the next meeting. The Presbyterian-Reformed theologians were concerned about how much flexibility there was in Roman Catholic dogmatic and doctrinal positions. (Interestingly, this basic question was asked of Roman Catholics in early sessions of dialogue on the Nicene Creed. The response of the late John Courtney Murray is published in the first volume of the Lutheran-Roman Catholic Consultation.[2]) The Roman Catholic theologians were concerned about how the Presbyterian-Reformed tradition maintained a dogmatic and doctrinal principle. So the topic chosen for further discussion was the development of doctrine.

The third meeting was October 27-30, 1966, in Chicago, Illinois. The papers presented were "The Development of Doctrine in Reformed Theology" by John Newton Thomas and "The Development and Reform of Doctrine" by Eugene M. Burke. Both these papers were published in *Reconsiderations*.[3] The Worship and Mission Section presented a study entitled "Dialogue: Common Worship and Study for Roman Catholics and Protestants—A Program of Peace, Prayer, and Praise for the Christian People," prepared by John Middaugh and Maurice Schepers. This study became the basic source for the common worship of the consultation.

At the end of the meeting we felt that we had established enough common ground to justify focusing on specific theological issues. As we saw it then, a basic obstacle to unity was the very diverse structure of ministry in the two traditions and especially the questions of episcopacy and papacy.

The fourth meeting was held April 26-29, 1967, at Collegeville, Minnesota. The papers presented to the Theological Section were "Order and Ministry in the Reformed Tradition" by Robert McAfee Brown and "The Ministry and Order of the Church" by Daniel O'Hanlon. These papers were also published in *Reconsiderations*.[4] Presented to the Worship and Mission Section were "Changes in Mixed Marriage" by J. C. Wynne and "The Holy Spirit in Worship and Witness" by Arthur C. Cochrane.

By the time of this meeting mutual trust and openness were growing into real friendship. Discussion was easy; sharp, even intense, questioning generated no heat and so the very thorny question of ministry opened areas and issues that could not have been handled before. As a result, it was decided that we should attempt a joint statement on ministry. Before the statement could be written, however, it was agreed that it should be divided into sections and each would be discussed in detail. So the first area of discussion would be ministry in general; only after consensus on that would we consider episcopacy and papacy. It was agreed that no papers would be presented at the next meeting but the issues on ministry raised at this meeting would be discussed in depth.

The fifth meeting was held October 26-29, 1967, in Lancaster, Pennsylvania. The atmosphere experienced at Collegeville continued to develop here. The discussion on ministry was extensive and fruitful enough to enable us to agree on preparing a tentative statement on the subject. This draft would be discussed at our next meeting and prepared for publication.

The sixth meeting was held May 9-11, 1968, at Bristow, Virginia. A joint statement on ministry was agreed upon. It was published in *Journal of Ecumenical Studies*.[5] Perhaps the most important part of this meeting was that in this place in rural Virginia we were thrown very much into each other's company. Out of this came the realization that the consultation had become a network of personal friendships. Looking back at the whole process, I have become convinced that there is no fully effective dialogue until the participants become friends, for friendship means love, trust, and commitment.

The seventh meeting was held October 24-27, 1968, at Allen Park, Michigan. The Theological Section had no papers but continued its discussions on the remaining areas of ministry. The Worship and Mission Section presented two papers: "The Churches and Their Attitude Toward Inter-Christian Marriages" by Glenn Baumann, subsequently published in *Worship*,[6] and "Proposed Pastoral Guidelines for Interchristian Marriages" by Henry Beck, also published in *Worship*.[7]

The eighth meeting was held May 21-24, 1969, at Charleston, South Carolina. Presented to the Theological Section were two papers: "Validation of Ministries in the New Testament" by John Charlot and "Ways of Validating Ministry" by Kilian McDonnell. The latter was published in *Journal of Ecumenical Studies*.[8] The Worship and Mission Section was presented a paper, "A Theological View of Christian Marriage," by Christopher Kiesling, subsequently published with modifications under the title "Light and Shadow."[9]

The ninth meeting was held October 30-November 1, 1969, at Macatawa, Michigan. For the Theological Section two papers were presented: "Apostles and Apostolic Succession in the Patristic Era" by James McHugh and "Report Concerning Office (General Synod: Reformed Church in Netherlands)" by Eugene Osterhaven. These papers and those in the previous meeting were asked for by the Theological Section to clarify, and give background to, issues raised in their discussions. In the Worship and Mission Section three papers were presented: "Divorce and Remarriage as Understood in the United Presbyterian Church" by Lewis Briner, "The Church and Second Marriage" by John Catoir, and "Recommendations for Changes Regarding Inter-Christian Marriage" by the Santa Barbara Workshop conducted by Ann Dunn.

At the final session of this meeting the Theological Section commissioned Ross Mackenzie and Eugene Burke to go through the papers and discussions on ministry and prepare a draft for a joint statement on all the sectors of ministry. This draft was to be ready for the next meeting.

The next meeting was held May 13-16, 1970, at Morristown, New Jersey. Prepared for the Theological Section was the draft proposal for a joint statement, "Ministry in the Church," which appeared in *Journal of Ecumenical Studies*.[10] The Worship and Mission Section was presented with a draft paper entitled "Joint Statement on Women in the Church and Ministry." Of significance here is the fact that this latter statement and much of its background had been shared with the Theological Section. Women invited to address the Worship and Mission Section on the topic of women also spoke to members of the Theological Section. A panel of women from different denominations addressed a joint session of the two sections and answered questions. As a result, the final statement of the Theological Section on ministry in the Church gave considerable emphasis to women in the Church. At this meeting a joint statement, "Women in the Church and Society," was approved; it appeared in *Journal of Ecumenical Studies*.[11]

The eleventh meeting was October 30-November 1, 1970, at Princeton, New Jersey. James Nichols presented a paper, "Episcopal/Presbyterian Polity," and he and Leonard Swidler presented a draft proposal on episcopacy. The role of the papacy was discussed at length and a broader view of the Church's ministry to the world was discussed in detail. The question of non-repetition of ordination in both traditions was raised in connection with the Roman Catholic doctrine of the sacramental "character" attributed to ordination. The question was resolved by having a Roman Catholic member and a Presbyterian-Reformed member formulate their respective positions in the footnotes. A statement on papal infallibility as currently understood was also discussed and a Roman Catholic member asked to formulate it in a footnote for the final statement.

The twelfth meeting was held May 11-14, 1971, at Columbus, Ohio. Presented to the Theological Section were two papers: "The Future of the Church, a Reformation Perspective" and "A More United Church of Christ for the Future" by Ross Mackenzie and Carl Peter respectively. The Worship and Mission Section was presented two papers with a view to a joint statement on women in the Church: "The Man-Woman Relationship as a Key to the Understanding of the New Humanity," and "Excerpts from the Report of the Task Force on Women Presented to the 183rd General Assembly, 1971."[12] The last detailed discussions on the joint statements of both sections took place.

The thirteenth meeting was October 27-30, 1971, at Richmond, Virginia. The statements of both sections of the consultation were finalized and approved for publication. The Worship and Mission Section's statement, "Women in the Church," was published in *Journal of Ecumenical Studies*.[13] The Theological Section's joint statement, "Ministry in the Church," was published in the same journal.[14]

A large portion of this meeting was devoted both formally and informally to the future of the consultation. It was recommended that the consultation should be restructured for its next stage and that its time should be limited. The general desire was to direct our efforts toward the ecumenical future. With this in mind, Daniel O'Hanlon presented a program which delineated what the consultation should seek to do in the next stage, which has now come to a conclusion after three years of work. The opening lines of O'Hanlon's proposal read: "The focus of its [the consultation's] work should be the concrete goal of the Christian unity of our churches. Its first task should be, in on-going dialogue, to describe as clearly as we can the shape of the unity we seek." In assenting to this proposal, the consultation asked its author to prepare a position paper on his proposal. The consultation also asked for data on the state of ecumenical cooperation in the United States.

The fourteenth meeting was October 27-30, 1972, in Cincinnati, Ohio. This was the first meeting of the restructured consultation. It was no longer divided into two sections but was one body with representatives from each general area, both old and new members, as well as representatives from the fields of Church history and sociology. It was not, however, a case of starting over again because many participants had shared the experience of the preceding years. Two papers were presented: "The Task Ahead— Some Observations for Discussion" by Daniel O'Hanlon and "A Report on Ecumenical Cooperation" by Nathan VanderWerf from the Commission on Regional and Local Ecumenism at the National Council of Churches.

Out of the discussion over these papers there gradually came to the fore the basic exigency and continuing problematic of our efforts to describe the shape of the unity we seek. The problem was how to keep an ecumenically sound theological perspective and yet give concrete form to the shape of the unity we seek; how to look beyond ecumenical cooperation and realistically envisage that unity which is the ultimate goal of ecumenism.

As the discussion developed, it became apparent that the group strongly felt its need for some experienced data about ecumenical activity at the "grass roots" level. On the basis of Nathan VanderWerf's report, Columbus, Ohio, was chosen as the place to gather this data. In Columbus was the Metropolitan Area Church Board, in which all the churches participated to initiate and encourage ecumenical activity. Columbus was the headquarters of the Ohio State Council of Churches, in which five out of seven Roman Catholic dioceses participated. Subsequently four members of the consultation agreed to form a task force to study the ecumenical situation in Columbus first-hand.

The fifteenth meeting, May 30-June 2, 1973, was at Columbus, Ohio. The discussion was divided into two parts. The first was on the reports of the task force regarding their experience in Columbus. The second part was on two papers: "The Shape of the Unity We Seek" by Eugene Burke and "Community and Institutional Factors in the Shape of the Unity We Seek" by Arleon Kelley. The first paper endeavored to explore the areas opened by contemporary Roman Catholic ecclesiology since Vatican II. Arleon Kelley's paper sought to formulate, in the disciplines and categories of sociology, the problems and obstacles to unity as well as the existing elements on which unity could be built. My own paper was very strongly influenced by the Columbus experience. As I saw it, there was ecumenical cooperation but no overriding concern for Church unity in Columbus, and this concern would not exist until that cooperation had sound theological roots.

The discussion of the two papers underlined the basic problematic mentioned above: How attain a balanced focus between the theological factors and the sociological factors? An additional challenge was the fact that we were projecting into a future many of whose elements could not be known. In the time at our disposal it was not possible to resolve all these problems, so it was decided to continue the discussion of the two papers at the next meeting.

The sixteenth meeting was held October 25-27, 1973, at Cincinnati, Ohio. The meeting addressed itself to a continuation of the effort to draw from the material at hand an effective statement on the shape of the unity we seek. A set of categories was developed under which the material could be organized. These categories were: the nature of the Church, structure in the Church, worship in the Church, and Christian belief. The consultation was divided into four groups to study each of these categories and present the results of their work at the next meeting.

The seventeenth meeting was held May 9-11, 1974, in Columbus, Ohio, and the eighteenth October 24-26, 1974, in Cincinnati,

Ohio. The internal reports circulated represented efforts to articulate the problems and answers pertinent to the four categories decided upon at the sixteenth meeting. The papers were: "The Local Church: A Personal View" by Sally Cunneen, "The Religious Group as Community" by Raymond Potvin, "The People of God as a Potential for Authentic Humanism" by Eugene Burke, "Toward the Unity We Seek in Worship" by Christopher Kiesling, "Christian Belief: Source of Unity and/or Division" by Leonard Swidler, "Liberation and Ministry of Women and Laity" by Margrethe Brown, "Report of Task Force on Structure" by Ross Mackenzie, and "Sociological Reflections on the Columbus Experience" by Raymond Potvin. The discussion on the papers was able to keep a fairly well-balanced focus on our basic problematic. Finally it was decided to ask Ross Mackenzie and Eugene Burke to formulate a joint statement incorporating the ideas in the papers developed in each of the four categories.

The nineteenth meeting of this consultation, the last of the second stage of its efforts, was held May 22-24, 1975, in Washington, D.C. The draft proposal was organized into four sections: I. The Mission and Nature of the One Church of Christ; II. The Structure of the One Church of Christ; III. The Worship of the One Church of Christ; IV. The Common Faith of the One Church of Christ. Each of these sections was gone over line by line by the whole consultation in joint session and appropriately revised. Only strictly editorial questions remained; Christopher Kiesling and John Beardslee III agreed to prepare a final redaction for signatures and publication.

Eugene M. Burke, C.S.P.

Notes

1. *Reconsiderations: Roman Catholic/Presbyterian and Reformed Theological Conversations 1966-67* (New York: World Horizons, Inc., 1967), pp. 13-45.
2. "The Status of the Nicene Creed as Dogma of the Church," in *Lutherans and Catholics in Dialogue,* I:16-30.

3. Pp. 49-104.

4. Pp. 107-58.

5. "The Ministry of the Church," *Journal of Ecumenical Studies* 5 (1968):462-65.

6. 42 (1968):609-16.

7. 43 (1969):159-65.

8. 7 (1970):209-65.

9. *Cross and Crown* 21 (1969):24-39.

10. 7 (1970):686-90.

11. *Ibid.*, pp. 690-91.

12. For a report on this meeting, see "Explosive Ecumenics," *Journal of Ecumenical Studies* 8 (1971):740.

13. 9 (1972):235-41. Also available from BCEIA, 1312 Massachusetts Ave., N.W., Washington, D.C. 20005, or Room 918, 475 Riverside Drive, New York, N.Y. 10027.

14. *Ibid.*, pp. 589-612. Also available from the sources mentioned in previous note.

THE UNITY WE SEEK

A Statement by the Roman Catholic/
Presbyterian-Reformed Consultation

I. THE MISSION AND NATURE OF THE ONE CHURCH OF CHRIST

"Christ is the visible likeness of the invisible God. He is the firstborn Son, superior to all created things. For by him God created everything in heaven and on earth, the seen and the unseen things, including spiritual powers, lords, rulers, and authorities. God created the whole universe through him and for him. He existed before all things, and in union with him all things have their proper place. He is the head of his body, the Church; he is the source of the body's life; he is the firstborn Son who was raised from death, in order that he alone might have the first place in all things. For it was by God's own decision that the Son has in himself the full nature of God. Through the Son, then, God decided to bring the whole universe back to himself. God made peace through his Son's death on the cross, and so brought back to himself all things, both on earth and in heaven" (Col. 1:15-20).

Proclaimed here is the complete sufficiency of Christ as the center of humanity's history and as the head of the Church. For the fullness of God, his wisdom and power are in Christ who shares these with the Church which, in turn, affects all humanity through the preaching of the Gospel. Thus the Church is the visible, historical, socially articulated manifestation of God's eternal decree in Christ. By that decree the Father calls all humanity to communion with himself, the Son, and the Spirit. The Church is willed and called into being to witness to this divine universal love and mercy. Hence by Word and sacrament, by every possible service of reconciliation, the Church must seek to be a sign of this mission and endeavor to accomplish it effectively.

11

Yet the existence of consultations such as ours sorrowfully testifies to the many failures of the Christian Church as it has sought to accomplish this mission. Consciousness of these evident failures led from the world mission movement to the ecumenical movement. This same deepening awareness has more and more permeated the discussions of the Roman Catholic/Presbyterian-Reformed Bilateral Consultation. This common conviction concerning the mission of the Church of Christ, the history of our bitter and rending discords, the vocation of the Church to be a sign of unity and a witness to God's love—all these have led us to choose the theme of this joint statement: the shape of the unity we seek.

The Problem

If we maintain—we believe we must—that ecclesial unity is possible, then can we describe this possibility realistically? Can we so give shape to this possibility of Christian unity that we will be able to state future goals with Christian realism? Our very existence as a consultation underlies our affirmative approach. This does not mean a claim to spell out each step. Nor does it mean that we can define in clear and complete detail a future Christian Church which is authentically one. What we do affirm is that in the present biblical, historical, theological, and sociological resources it is possible to construct a working model that can be projected into the future.[1] In taking this theme we are aware that we are undertaking to come to grips with the ultimate concern of ecumenism as well as of this consultation. Basically our theme entails a real response to the question: What do we mean when we say "one Church"? It also obliges us to try to describe in the concrete the ecclesial unity we seek.

The People of God

Our consensus is that the first step in understanding the shape of the unity we seek is an understanding of the Church as the people of God. In treating the Church as the people of God we realize that it is only one aspect of the total mystery of the Church of Christ. By beginning with this dimension, however, we intend to give primacy to what is the beginning and abiding core of the Christian life—our oneness in Christ through faith and baptism. It affirms that this faith and baptism are the cause and initiation of our unity; any distinction is subordinate to this unity and to be judged by the priority of our commitment to Christ. Accepting the Church as the people of God also puts in the forefront one of the basic characteristics of biblical revelation—the corporate or communal character of salvation. Finally, it gives strong stress to the visible historical character of God's Church and the historical character of God's dialogue with his people. So it points firmly to the role of historical event and human experience—the historicity of man—in God's salvific design.

Our understanding of the Church as the people of God is rooted in both Testaments. St. Paul begins with the idea of Israel as the people of God. It is a people chosen by God and given his covenanted promises and love. Yet, as prophetically understood, it is imperfect, awaiting a new and universal covenant in the future. So, for St. Paul, the Church is the new people, linked with Israel but founded by Jesus Christ, ministering to the advance of God's reign and the salvation and reconciliation of all humanity. It has been called together through Christ and is an essential element of God's plan of salvation. It possesses a new covenant that consecrates this new people to God. Like Israel, it too is imperfect, a "pilgrim Church," beset by historical tensions and the weakness of the flesh, but, "moved by the Spirit, it may never cease to renew itself until through the cross it arrives at that light that knows no setting."[2]

To this new people of God the Spirit gives his gifts in abundance, because this whole people shares the prophetic office of Christ. Each member is called to be a living witness through a life of faith and love. All the gifts are given for the building up of the Church. Each member has a Christian ministry. Each ministry is a gift of the Spirit. Each ministry has a necessary role to play in the wholeness of the unity of the Church.[3] The ultimate quality of these gifts is the love that informs and motivates them.[4] These charisms are a continuing reality and an integral dimension of the structure of the Church. In affirming this Pauline doctrine we are only reaffirming a basic element of his ecclesiology and so more effectively indicating the shape of the unity we seek.[5]

Implicit in an ecclesiology modeled on the people of God of

the new covenant is the principle of catholicity. For this people of God of the new covenant *is* the principle of catholicity. This new people of God looks to all humanity, since the reason for this people's existence in Jesus Christ is to be a bearer of the good news to all humanity. Thus we cannot attempt to define the future unless we also affirm that diversity and unity are not mutually exclusive. Pluralism is endemic to human beings and has richly positive dynamisms and creative possibilities. So also for God's people. Diversities of language, of culture, of religious and historical experience are not by nature divisive. Rather they are called to be part of a rich and manifold expression of that total reality of our reconciliation with God in Christ.

In saying this, however, we must contritely take into full account our Christian past and present and so our failure to live with diversity. We must acknowledge that the power of religious passion has again and again created a mentality that looks upon any diversity as contrary to the will of Christ. Yet, if we are to give a future unity shape, we are convinced that we must also accept diversity on many levels and in many aspects. Otherwise our goal is impossible, and this we as Christians do not believe.

In the light of this principle of catholicity, we propose for consideration the theological tentative of a typology of churches.[6] "Type" (*typos*) here means general form or character. The assertion is that there can be a plurality of types (*typoi*) within the communion of the church of Christ. In the words of Cardinal Willebrands: ". . . the notion . . . of a *typos* of a Church does not primarily designate a diocese or a national church. . . . It is a notion which has its own phenomenological aspects with their own theological meaning."[7] Thus, "where there is a long, coherent tradition commanding men's [and women's] love and loyalty, creating and sustaining a harmonious and organic whole of complementary elements, each of which supports and strengthens the other, you have the reality of a *typos*."[8]

We see, then, as the shape of our future unity, a communion of communions (*communio communiorum*), a Church of churches (*Ecclesia ecclesiarum*), each communion in the whole being a living, historical community gathered together in the name of Christ by faith and baptism. Each gathering has a tradition that embodies an enduring Christian commitment and an experience proper to itself. Out of this comes a theological, liturgical, and spiritual tradition which is accepted by the community and through which the community endeavors to live the Christian life. Each communion, as the whole Christian Church, accepts as the wellspring of its unity and the heart of its common loyalty the person and message of Jesus Christ and the graced conviction that he is God and Savior.

Our mutual conviction is that the shape of unity conceived in terms of a communion of communions is a very fruitful approach to future unity. It avoids the abstraction of a superchurch that transcends all diversities and denominationalism. Such an abstraction tends to ignore the continuing human experience of catholicity. We are sharply aware from historical experience that this approach of a communion of communions has its own dangers. Excessive denominationalism and consequent sectarianism must be constantly guarded against. As has been pointed out to us, denominationalism can readily involve "misconstrued priorities" whereby the denomination is first and the Church is second.[9] Denominationalism leads to a strong negative reaction to any larger, positive overseeship. History also makes us aware that large-scale oversight runs the real danger of negating diversity and emphasizing uniformity for the sake of efficiency and unanimity of action.

While we have chosen the model of the Church as the people of God as primary to our ecumenical purpose, we recognize that it cannot totally suffice for the full explicitation of our theme. For the emphasis on this dimension of the Church's visible and historical character and its catholicity may well obscure the transcendent unity of all Christians. For what distinguishes the unity of the Christian community from any other community is that it is the body of Christ—another Pauline model. In this latter model we see the divine life revealed in Jesus Christ and communicated to believers by the Holy Spirit. The Christian Church, of course, has visible and social bonds, but the bonds are engendered by the spiritual community of grace and charity by which Christ becomes the head of the Church, his body. This spiritual bond constitutes the whole Christ—head and members.

Sign of the Unity of All Humanity

As we have reflected together on our common quest for unity, it has become increasingly evident that the unity Christ willed for his Church he also willed for all humanity. As Christians, we believe that Christ's redemptive mission encompasses the entire human community. In this belief so many in the ecumenical movement find their most powerful motivation that Christian unity may be the harbinger of that peace and unity it seeks to promote. For this reason we see the Church as called to be a sign—a sacrament —of that unity which God has willed for his creation and disclosed in Jesus Christ. Yet, again, we have been confronted with the history of our separations and divisions and the tragic sign that they are. We must acknowledge that only God's grace can make us the instrument of unity. Nonetheless, this very consciousness of our failure has animated our efforts toward unity. At this moment we see Christians as having a charismatic ministry to press toward unity with every effort. It becomes, then, an integral part of the Christian vocation to pray and to demand that Christian leaders will work together to unite the Church of Christ, so that it will become a fruitful sign and instrument of that unity to which God has called the total human family.

As part of the total human community, the ministry of the Church must play a real and vital role in the needs of that community. In the grim actualities of our day, the public proclamation of the need for peace and justice does not suffice. Oppression, lack of education, malnutrition, and famine are not abstractions but agonizing and mortal problems in our own nation and in the world community.

We must not forget that these problems have found their most tragic and complex dimensions in countries that have been the object of Christian missionary effort for generations and even centuries. Here in a special way the Church is called to be not only a sign but an effective bearer of hope, performing a Christian ministry of reconciliation. But we Christians will not be able to effectuate such a ministry unless first of all we show ourselves aware that we have failed in many ways. Perhaps unwittingly and despite good intentions, all too often Christian missionaries have become instruments of colonial establishments. We realize that we cannot begin over again, but we also see that evangelical realism must accept the principle of catholicity.

A genuine and unmistakable commitment to the concrete

human needs of our day is an inescapable obligation of the Christian Church seeking for unity. Only when this commitment is evident to what has been called the Third World can the Church effectively carry out its ministry of reconciliation and become a prophet of a better hope.

This ministry of reconciliation must witness that the dynamic power of an authentic Christian ministry to human needs is the proclamation of the person and message of Jesus Christ. It is the crucified and risen Christ that we must preach if humanity's hope is to be engendered. Under no circumstances should the Church appear as just another social agency. But to proclaim the Gospel with believable conviction and authenticity, we need to show ourselves committed to giving concrete form to the evangelical imperatives of freedom, justice, peace, and mutual love.

A Pilgrim Church

Finally, in our general thematic—the shape of the unity we seek—we are cognizant of the eschatological nature of the Church and its mission. We accept the fact that the Christian Church is a pilgrim Church always in need of reform and renewal. Hence, we must view the Church in the eschatological perspectives of salvation history. "The unity and catholicity of the Church are always and in every case in process; they will always remain a task. The solution cannot lie either in mutual absorption or in a simple integration of individual Christian communities but only in the constant conversion of all, that is, in the readiness to let the event of unity, already anticipated in grace and sign, occur over and over again in obedience to the one Gospel as the final norm in and over the Church."[10]

II. THE UNITY WE SEEK IN BELIEF

As Christians we all believe it has been divinely revealed that Jesus is God and Savior, sent by the Father to lead all creation under the guidance of the Spirit to salvation,[11] to liberation,[12] "to reconcile everything in his person" (Col. 1:20). Our trust in Jesus assures us that God the Father has sent him, and still continues to work through him in the power of the Spirit.

In this or a like statement we have the two basic elements of our Christian belief, our creed. One element is the act *by which (fides qua)* we articulate our faith, namely, our trusting in Jesus and God the Father through the power of the Spirit. This is our "faith as act." The second element is that *about which (fides quae)* we affirm our trust, namely, that Jesus is God and Savior and so forth. This is our "faith as content."

All Christians clearly have the first element, the faith as act, in common. All also doubtless have the fundamental portions of the second element, the faith as content, in common. But because the Christian community (the Church) was from the beginning a living community, that is, a community which attempted to live according to its beliefs, it naturally reflected on the faith as content in light of its on-going living experience, applied it to that experience with varying success, and handed on *(tra-ditio)* the results of its reflections and applications.[13] Hence, the faith as content— those things which Christians trusted that God the Father had done in Jesus for us, those "truths" of the faith—became ever more refined and applied.

In time and in space not all Christians agreed fully on all such refinements and applications. When this lack of agreement reached sufficient intensity, the unity of the faith was rent, that is, in effect one group of Christians stated that another group's lack of affirming certain "essential" elements of the faith as content was so fundamental as to seem to imply that their trusting in God, their faith as act, was also essentially not Christian. But it is impossible for one group of Christians to assert with certitude that only they are in good faith, that is, have an authentic faith as act, as trust in God. Yet it is to such an attempt that we Christians, including Reformed and Roman Catholic Christians, have often turned.

To regain an essential Christian unity in the areas of belief, all Christians must first clearly recognize and affirm that all Christians "in good faith" do indeed share the same trust in God who has wrought all creation's liberation in Jesus, the same faith as act. With this mighty fulcrum of a consciously shared faith in Christ (faith as act), we Christians should be able to remove all obstacles to essential Christian unity resulting from reflections on, and applications of, the faith as content.

What Is Essential in Christian Belief?

Central in Christian belief is Jesus as God and Savior. Outside of the first witnesses, all Christians come to know Jesus through the Christian proclamation, the Christian story; Paul says that we come to faith through hearing (Rom. 10:17). Here then is the common essential core of our Christian belief—the person of Jesus as handed on ("traditioned") through the Christian story as told primarily in the Scriptures and reverberated subsequently in various Christian communities throughout history.

But when Christians move beyond perceiving Jesus as God and Savior through the Christian story and attempt to live according to this perception, that is, attempt to say in their own actions and words what they understand, then human, historical, cultural conditions and limitations enter visibly. Indeed, they were necessarily present from the beginning of Christian belief, for there can be no talk of the perception of Jesus as God and Savior except in terms of the dialectic of the perceiver and the perceived. But when the perceiver, here the Christian believer, takes the next step and expresses what he or she perceives, believes, then naturally the particular stance of the perceiver (believer) essentially affects the statements (beliefs, creeds).

Of course, some persons and groups have greater clarity and strength of perception (belief) on some issues than others, and some have more effective powers of expression (statement of "truths," creeds) than others. Hence the statements of belief or creeds (faith as content) of such Christians will come to be seen by the community, or large portions of it, as helpful expressions of the reflections on, and applications of, the Christian story which echo the more or less unexpressed perceptions, beliefs, of the less articulate members of the community. Not all such statements will be equally helpful to all Christians of all times and places.

This kind of relativity is not only not surprising, but even greatly to be desired. Each individual and each community of Christians could be satisfied with simply repeating identically the same statements of other Christian communities only if their experienced situation in the world were totally the same as that of the other groups. This is a clear impossibility since every individual and every community is unique in a significant sense. If the revelation that Jesus is God and Savior is to affect the lives of Christians, individually and communally, Christians must reflect on and apply what they have perceived and believed. When the stance in the world of enough Christians changes sufficiently, they will naturally feel the need to express proportionately their new perception (belief) in communal fashion in accordance with their new situation.

All this quite naturally happens not only to individuals and small groups of Christians, but also to large communities within the universal Church, and at times even to the whole Church, as it moves through history. This trusting response of faith (faith as act) on the part of the Christian Church, or large portions of it, spells out through a variety of organs the newly perceived or newly applied dimensions (faith as content) of the Christian revelation at various times and places in Christian history, leading the community of believers, the Church, to an ever richer expression of the Christian faith. Christians trust that this process occurs under the guidance of the Spirit, who is the Spirit of truth and, as Jesus promised, "will guide you unto all the truth" (Jn. 16:13). This growth is what theologians refer to as development of doctrine.

Handling Differences of Belief

But such new expressions (creeds, theologies) need not mean the rejection of other expressions that were, or are, found helpful by other groups of Christians, or by the same group at another time.[14] Christians would do well to seek the truth wherever they can find it, that is, in this context, seek that which is helpful in the Christian statements of belief of other Christians. This approach would eliminate many, if not most, of the obstacles to essential Christian unity arising from differences in beliefs (faith as content). However, if the differences become so fundamental as to seem to approach mutual exclusivity, then an effective means must be found which would allow (indeed, facilitate) all Christians to arrive at an expression of Christian belief that will be acceptable, that is, truly helpful, to all.

For several centuries after the beginning of the fourth century A.D., the ecumenical councils seemed to be a more or less effective instrument for resolving conflicts, although they were not without their faults of polemics, schisms, and other scandals. Perhaps the insights of group dynamics and the broader and longer experience in representative and participatory democratic procedures and structures of the modern period would help to make councils an even more effective means of arriving at generally (ecumenically) helpful expressions of Christian belief. So also would the newly developed cross-fertilization of Protestant and Roman Catholic Scripture scholarship, which would greatly facilitate the testing of all faith statements against the original Christ event as revealed and "traditioned" in the Scriptures. So too would the Roman Catholic insight that there is a hierarchy of doctrine, whereby certain faith affirmations provide the perspective within which other faith elements are to be understood and interpreted[15]—an insight very like that of "the core of the Gospel"[16] of the Reformed tradition. At any rate, such an instrument or instruments must be sought and then constantly employed and improved.

Our two Christian traditions, Roman Catholic and Reformed, have in their history several communal statements of Christian belief of accepted major significance. Some are held jointly from the earlier centuries of the history of the Christian Church, for example, the Apostles' Creed and the Nicene Creed; some are held separately, for example, the creedal portions of the Council of Trent for Roman Catholics, the Westminster Confession, Heidelberg Catechism, Second Helvetic Confession, and the Confession of 1967 for the Reformed. Such major expressions of Christian belief, and others not listed here, should be cherished as a sacred trust in our Christian heritage and should be used as wellsprings of an ever deeper and broader understanding of the Christ event. Surely this is true of the mutually shared creedal statements and the statements of one's own tradition; but can and should it not also be true of most of the other traditions' statements as well?

An intense study of the faith statements of both traditions undertaken jointly would probably show that there is a vast area of congruence and a further large area of mutually inclusive complementarity. If significant elements still appeared to remain mutually exclusive, they could then be presented to the accepted instruments designed to resolve creatively such oppositions, for example, local, regional, national, and international dialogue groups, and ultimately a fully ecumenical, that is, universal, council.

Indeed, in an extremely important manner this has already been taking place. It is most apparent in the joint statements issued by dialogue groups such as this one,[17] and other consultations.[18] But the reconciliation of portions of faith statements which previously appeared mutually exclusive has also been occurring internally in the sense that the separate traditions have themselves moved beyond the positions of certain earlier perceptions. For example, the papacy is no longer described as the anti-Christ in all official versions of the Westminster Confession,[19] and the Roman Catholic Church officially no longer refuses to refer to Protestant communities as churches.[20] This process needs to be broadened, deepened, and accelerated.

Thus, seen in historical perspective, the creedal statements of the Christian Church, and specifically our Roman Catholic and Reformed communions, fall largely into three periods: first, jointly held statements, then separately held statements, and now in part jointly and in part separately held statements. It is hoped that this period will give way to a fourth, and last, period of statements held jointly on an even more profound level.

We see then the kind of unity in the area of belief that is essential to a united Christian Church to be one which recognizes and encourages a multiplicity of mutually complementary statements of faith (and the many theological cultures, that is, patterns of worship, Church structures, styles of living, etc., that will reflect, and in turn will affect, them). At the same time this unity must also work through effective instruments at first to hold apparently mutually exclusive basic elements in a creative tension, and eventually to reconcile them. Important touchstones in this creative process of reconciliation would be the *whole* Scripture, the *whole* tradition, and the voice of the *whole* contemporary living Church. This insistence on wholeness will be the safeguard against heresy, which is a "choosing of a part."

Recommendations

This consultation, therefore, recommends to its parent bodies, the National Conference of Catholic Bishops and the North American Area of the World Alliance of Reformed Churches, that they commission a thoroughgoing scholarly study of each other's major faith statements, as well as the various subsequent internal revisions and joint statements, with a view to analyzing them as described above, that is, into those elements which are held jointly, those which are complementary, and those which appear to be mutually exclusive. The team of scholars appointed would have to include at least one Reformed and one Roman Catholic Christian for each statement chosen to be studied. The results of these studies should then be both sent to the parent bodies with recommendations for actions and also filtered into all the levels of the several churches' educational operations from that of the preschool through the parish, adult education, college, and the seminary.

This consultation also wishes to urge all Roman Catholic and Reformed scholars, clergy, and laity to begin immediately or to continue to take up these joint studies of each other's understandings of faith on all levels, whether in congregational study groups, clergy dialogue groups, university sponsored symposia, councils of churches' projects, or other forums. Only thus can all Christians fully reflect on and apply their faith to their living.

III. THE UNITY WE SEEK IN STRUCTURE

What we say about the unity of the Church must be translated into specific recommendations concerning its structures. In the process of convergence each church will bring to this unity the distinctive richness of its own experience and hope. The Spirit will enable the churches to grow together as they come closer. Our task now is to clarify the process by which we may move toward unity in structure.

The center of the Church's unity and life is Jesus, who is God's self-disclosure and therefore our Lord and Savior. For this reason we seek to conform all the structures of our faith and life to his mind and Gospel, not modeling ourselves on the world around us but by the new mind that we have received from him. Our starting point is, therefore, our readiness for that repentance which is critical reflection upon our previous practices and the renewed orientation of all our structures to the mind and Gospel of Christ.

Principles for a Period of Transition

In passing from our present structures to those future forms which are not yet clear to us, we can roughly indicate a direction which reflects our separated pasts as well as our common hope, our disparate traditions as well as our shared future. The following principles are offered as guidelines for those changes for which we can hope. But we must also be alert to discern the prophetic word and act for which we have not prepared, and the sign which has not been reckoned on.

The first need is to plan for a period of gradual transition, reflection, and shared experience. In this process the whole Church must examine not only the depths that it sees in "the mystery of Christ" (Eph. 3:4) but also the social reality which likewise belongs to its nature in history; not only its mission to the world but also what has been grasped and lived out and is being embodied in concrete new patterns of life together.

The process should occur at all levels. The entire Church should be prepared to accept and advocate this transition, reflection, and experience. Initiatives taken at the local level are of first importance. A unique responsibility therefore resides in the local church, in full consultation with the other local churches of the ecclesiastical province or judicatory. Any change that is going to take place will involve an interchange between various manifestations of the Church, in the local congregations as well as at regional, national, and ecumenical or world levels. Any initiatives or changes that help to achieve the transition or broaden the shared experience should be permitted and encouraged, where they are found to be appropriate.

Since the Church is summoned to reveal to the world the mystery of Christ, *all its structures are to be subordinated to the mission of the Son and of the Holy Spirit.* In the biblical witness the Spirit is both a divine, dynamic force as well as the principle of life and activity proper to the Christian. There is therefore both an interior and exterior relation between the Spirit and Church order. The Spirit has many fruits, and the structures of the Church, as it passes through a period of transition to a fullness of unity, will be fruitful as they create the ministries by which the mission of the Church is carried out. The mission and the structures of the

Church are integral to one another. In the period of transition our concern with structures flows from our call to discipleship among all peoples.

The catholicity of the Church implies and is properly expressed in a communion of communions. Within the organic whole of the one Church there are and always have been complementary elements or empirically contributory factors, each of which supports and strengthens the others. These elements are the living, historical Christian communities gathered in the name of Christ, each with its tradition that articulates its faith and hope and its experience proper to itself.

Christian experience in contemporary cultures, and nowhere more than in the United States, has shown that, while pluralism has its own inherent dangers, it is inherent in our society with its diversity, conflict, and enrichment. With appropriate translations, we can expect a like pluralism within the Church. Indeed, the pluralism which we already see within the various communions indicates that we can expect a comparable pluralism within the coming Church. This suggests to us that we need to keep open to diversity of structure, while conserving those forms that are needed and effective.

The shape of the unity we seek will be wrought out in both freedom and order. The complexity and fragmentation of the world is for us the given situation, the milieu within which we shall move to new structures. What is called for is that we respond to the impulse of the Spirit which will enable us to break free of many of our present structures. The Spirit can never be contained.

The Church as a social system is also an orderly vehicle by which people are nurtured in their participation in God's act of creating and reintegrating the world. It is a social entity with all the human infrastructures that make up the whole. Unfailingly present, therefore, are the dynamisms and laws which make up the structure of the Church, with all its ambivalences and ambiguities. Tensions may lead to conflicts between freedom and orderliness, to disagreement and division especially on moral issues and long-range policies. But the tensions may also be positive goods. Because the Church is a human structure it will show political divisions. A society that looks for unanimous consent on all points at issue is artificial or moribund. A lively society should expect to see strong differences, and these differences need not necessarily rend its unity. Indeed, where there are no clearly articulated divisions in the freedom of the Gospel, we can suspect that they are being either stifled or driven below the surface.

This structure of freedom and order will typically be seen in its local manifestations. The task of leadership within the Church will be to facilitate this growth, not to oppose it, and to link it with other creative expressions in such a way that a larger unity may emerge. In the unity we seek, structures will not have firm and unyielding boundaries, but will aid the churches to see their relation to a common center. Often it may appear that the Church at a local level is hindered by people of narrow vision. But their focus on the local level may be a strength as much as a weakness. Faith, hope, and love always have to be translated into common words and actions. If they cannot be expressed in such daily concerns as job or family, they have no meaning. So the boundaries of which we speak, though discernible, should be regarded as flexible rather than as fixed. To be sure, the Church must have an articulated, corporate, and visible reality to it. God has really called us to redemption in Christ. If ever the Church is to have an impact on its members, it will be through its identity as the body of Christ. Yet we must always be concerned not only with the articulated center but also with the boundaries where we stand beside those who are in quest of a meaning for their lives.

How Can We Make the Transition?

What measures can the churches begin to take at present in changing, adapting, or modifying their structures? Our separate traditions and histories provide us already with patterns of Church order from which we may draw guiding principles. The patterns which we have known and used, even of irreducible ecclesial elements, are partial and transient. In ever fresh obedience to Christ we must open them to reflect the ecumenical character of the world mission of the Word of God. As the Church lives in preparation for the Advent presence of Christ, it becomes more ready to alter what is essentially incomplete in its structural forms.

A first stage in the transition to the fullness of Church unity should be a continuing process of general and comprehensive ecu-

menical consultation. The ecumenical movement of the modern period has been one of the decisive factors in our common life as Christians. Only if all the churches are committed to one another and determined by the Word of God can they address the theological questions about human existence and the ecclesial questions about Church structures.

Joint studies of movements for human liberation in and beyond the churches can foster imaginative action in hard or intractable problems. Collaboration in the concerns of fairness and equity in government, economic life, education, and the administration of justice can engender cooperation also in Church reform and renewal.

We can also pray together and for one another. A sign of this commitment to one another could be a covenanting agreement between particular churches in city, rural, or suburban areas to do as much together as possible. Two or more parishes, entering into conversation with one another, yoke themselves together in a common covenant. They may work together, for example, on a joint statement of their common faith. They may witness together by deed and word to the Gospel of the saving presence, activity, and teaching of the Lord. We also need agencies to deal with these questions at all levels beyond the local.

In various ways we seek possibilities of deepening trust in one another and learning from one another. Again at a local level, Roman Catholic and Presbyterian-Reformed churches could plan to let a given number of people, selected by their pastors, meet together regularly for a year to share their thoughts and hopes on the meaning of Christian faith and life today. Such an undertaking would not only be a real step, taken in the light of our commitment to the people of God, but would also help us to come to understand one another better. At such meetings the central question might be: What is so basic in our faith that we must pass it on to others?

Another stage in the transition will be a time of coalescence of ecclesial and organizational styles. Various styles of Church order and organization will be necessary for the life of the Church in a pluralistic society.

In the Reformed churches, the ministers of the Word exercise a corporate authority in worship, doctrine, and discipline, along with lay elders associated with them. In the courts of the churches, they together maintain continuity of ordination and jurisdiction. In the Roman Catholic Church, the hierarchical structures of orders and of Petrine and episcopal ministries are constitutive elements of the people of God, along with the renewed principles of collegiality and subsidiarity, as the sign of salvation in the world. These divergencies, which have caused separation in the past, may also, nevertheless, be a means of movement along fresh lines in the future. On the Reformed side there is a growing willingness on the part of many to discuss the corporate functioning of the Church in worship, doctrine, and pastoral oversight through a creative fusing of the episcopal, presbyteral, and congregational traditions. On the Roman Catholic side there have been great efforts to emphasize the role of the papacy as one of unity through service, carried out in collegiality with ever more levels of the Church.

There is abundant agreement in this consultation about the changes to which we are willing to come as a result of our living together. We can collaborate already in planning for change and improvement. We can share a number of ministries already. To become socialized into any kind of Christian community implies more than a matter of rational understanding. It is the acceptance and experiencing of the Christian faith in symbolic ways through rite and Church order. Among the Reformed and Presbyterian churches an increase in the number of eucharistic observances would be of significance in the course of our growing together. The Roman Catholic Church has much to learn from the experience of lay representation and government in the other communions.

Recommendations

In our approach to the unification of structure through the acceptance of a pluralism of ecclesial and organizational styles and mutual adaptation, members of this consultation refer to the recommendations which were appended to the statement made by the Theological Section of this consultation on October 30, 1971. These are:

A. That this Statement on Ministry in the Church be received and acted upon appropriately.

B. That proper steps be taken to have the appropriate organs of our respective churches at the highest level officially affirm in some appropriate way that Christ is present and at work in the ministries and Eucharist of each of our traditions.

C. That although *general* eucharistic sharing is not to be recommended for the present, these same appropriate organs designate *specific* occasions on which invitations to a eucharistic sharing may be extended.

D. That areas of ministry be opened, as far as possible, to qualified women, and that a major effort be undertaken to place qualified women, ordained and unordained, in offices and positions of leadership and decision-making; accordingly, that an ecumenical commission composed of women and men be constituted by our churches: to study the role of women in Church and society, especially the full involvement of women in all offices and leadership functions, both clerical and lay; to recommend corrective and innovative actions and programs in these areas; and to monitor their implementation.

E. That encouragement be given to explorations at the parish, diocesan, national, and world levels which would further the *practical* fusing, both within and between our churches, of the unifying role of individual leadership in service and of collegial, democratic responsibility, and that appropriate groups be commissioned both within and between our churches to implement this recommendation.

F. That effective Church action be taken to initiate or to intensify and broaden ecumenical learning and experiences on the grass-roots level, so that the lives of all of our Church members may be touched and significantly changed by the movement toward Christian understanding and unity; that committees which would provide effective programming in this area be set up or strengthened both on the national and local levels; specifically, that on the Roman Catholic side, the Committee on Education for Ecumenism of the Bishops' Committee on Ecumenical and Interreligious Affairs be reactivated to work closely with appropriate ecumenical education and programming committees of the Presbyterian-Reformed churches.

G. That an ecumenical consultation be constituted among our churches, and perhaps others, which would investigate basic moral issues of our time and ascertain as clearly as possible what the Christian Gospel has to say to them, such a consultation to be composed of women and men with the necessary range of experience, knowledge, and concern, among them persons with expertise in such areas as ethics, Scripture, theology, history, psychology, sociology, and political science.

H. That an ecumenical commission be constituted by our churches to study the evangelical values both of celibacy and of a married clergy.[21]

Ways of Expressing Structural Unity

On both sides we see the goal as that of realizing ecclesial and eucharistic communion. The goal is not unattainable. Many positive influences have helped us to lose suspicions and gain a sense of what it means for the pilgrim Church to live in the time between what has come and what has yet to come. Warm and cordial relations have developed between us, awareness of the catholicity we share has deepened, and our experience has convinced us that the oneness of Christ's Church must be demonstrated in fact.

The acceptance of one another's members. As they prepare themselves for a fullness of relationship between all the people of God, the churches meanwhile seek to bring their members into mutual acceptance of one another. The Church of the future may be expected to be "a communion of communions," and there is likely to emerge a variety of worshiping communities, liturgical styles, and modes of response to ethical issues. Appropriate discussion should take place within and beyond the churches about both the possibilities and the limits of such freedom.

The responsibility of all Christians for the life of the church. No group can function for long effectively without organization. People do not move purposefully in any direction unless their resources are channeled and directed by a leadership that includes both the creative enthusiasts and the bureaucrats. Though impor-

tant, efficient administration may be less so than the task of sym-
bolizing the goals and values of an organization in its very structure. In all the churches today the tasks of forming, serving,
developing, and integrating a Christian community require a variety of forms of leadership.

Increasingly, the people of God in the local community are
coming to experience and express the priestly and prophetic function and the participation in God's reign which they have received
from Christ. At each level in the life of the Church they are making their own decisions. A much more thorough reform of the
structures of communication and decision-making is necessary in
order that a full representation of those who are involved, women
and men alike, may replace authoritarian exercise of power. No
one group or person is in charge without qualification. Thus leadership is increasingly shared in the churches today: goals are set
out of the needs and perceptions of what is at issue and what are
the priorities. This increased emphasis on shared authority and the
real needs of the churches imply that the people of God in a particular place (the parish or congregation, the diocese or region)
participate fully both in leadership and in the choice of leaders.

The ordained ministry. Within the general ministry of the
whole Church, ministers are called and ordained to represent
Christ to the community and the community before Christ.
Through the proclamation of the Gospel and the celebration of the
sacraments this ministry has endeavored to unite and order the
Church for the ministry of the whole people of God. Setting a person apart for this ministry situates that person in the community
of the whole priestly people. It confers a special mission for the
sake of that community, viz., the building up of the community.

The function of the ordained ministry is to see to it that the
Word of God is proclaimed, the sacraments celebrated, individuals
led to Christian maturity, and the Christian community built up.
He or she may not necessarily do all of these things personally, but
is publicly responsible in view of ordination for seeing to it that
they are done. Each member of the Church is thus encouraged to
use the gift or gifts which the Spirit bestows on each one for the
edification of the whole body of Christ.

Apostolic succession and primacy. The Church is apostolic in that it lives the faith of the apostles and continues the mission which Christ gave to the apostles. The canonical Scriptures are the normative expression of this apostolicity. Within the general ministry of the whole Church the setting apart of some to the administration of the Word and sacrament includes the invocation of the Holy Spirit and the laying on of hands by other ordained ministers. The continuity of this special ministry of Word and sacrament arises in Christ's original commission to the apostles but depends also on his continual call and action. The invocation of the Holy Spirit reminds us that Jesus Christ is present and at work through the continual operation of his Holy Spirit. The laying on of hands is an effective sign that initiates and confirms the believer in the ministry which is conferred.

We believe in apostolic succession within the Church, though from our different standpoints we locate that succession in different ways. Apostolic succession consists at least in the continuity of the apostles' teaching, and this understanding is not in opposition to the idea of succession through continuity of ordained ministry. The two elements already described both inhere in apostolic succession: historical continuity with the apostles and the contemporary action of Christ through the Holy Spirit.

There are two main aspects of the papacy with which the Reformed churches have had difficulty: its claims to primacy and universal jurisdiction in Church government, and to infallibility in teaching. Our earlier statement of October 30, 1971 thus summarizes our discussion of these questions:

> The growing awareness in the Reformed churches of the need for effective worldwide unifying forms, and in Roman Catholicism of the collegial context and pastoral character of the papal role, opens the way to new possibilities in the first problem area. On the local level the contemporary Church needs a creative fusing of the episcopal and presbyteral/congregational traditions. So, too, on a much wider scale the Church needs, in a spirit of pastoral service, to blend the unifying drive which a papacy of the future might provide, with the vitalizing growth which can come from the "collegial" or represen-

tative spirit inherent in the Reformed tradition. Hence, one of the main questions may prove to be how effectively the conciliar and representative pattern can be fused at the world level with individual personal leadership. There will also need to be careful exploration as to precisely what kinds and what degree of ecclesiastical jurisdication are appropriate at each level: regional, national, and worldwide. Consequently, although our churches are presently divided in habits of thought and practice, as is true of both Roman Catholics and Presbyterian-Reformed Christians among themselves, it is clearly to the advantage both of the universal Church and also of the world to which it witnesses and ministers that we learn from each other and act jointly in this regard.[22]

IV. The Unity We Seek in Worship

The major features of the shape of the unity we seek in worship are: (1) recognition of a plurality of forms of worship as authentically Christian, (2) new communities of worship, (3) active participation of all, and (4) integrity of Christian worship. These features are explained in the following paragraphs.

1. *Recognition of a plurality of forms of worship as authentically Christian.* By "plurality of forms" we do not mean simply various services of worship such as baptism, the Eucharist, confirmation, proclamation of the Word, morning prayer, and so forth. Assuming these, we intend primarily a variety of forms resulting from different experiences and understandings of Christian faith and acceptable within individual Christian traditions. Thus there should be forms of worship reflecting the Roman Catholic tradition, the Presbyterian-Reformed tradition, and other Christian traditions, both Eastern and Western. One communion should recognize as authentically Christian the worship of another communion —for example, the Roman Catholic Church should recognize the worship of the Presbyterian-Reformed churches and vice versa. Within each communion there should be willingness to adopt new forms of worship in keeping with its tradition. There should also be newly created ecumenical forms in which all communions can recognize authentic Christian worship.

Such a plurality of forms of worship is justifiably expected. The New Testament bears witness to slightly different forms of eucharistic celebration.[23] Free prayer seems to have been especially vigorous in Pauline churches.[24] Whatever the New Testament evidence, the history of the Church provides ample witness to a multiplicity of liturgies. Theology testifies that this plurality of forms serves to bring out the richness of God's revelation in Jesus Christ, facilitates appropriation of revelation through faith by men and women of diverse cultures, and enables men and women to express their faith in worship suited to their mentality and needs.

Those forms which meet the criteria for the authenticity and integrity of Christian worship should be recognized in the unity we seek. This recognition should be official, that is, explicitly and formally stated by the competent overseeing persons or bodies of each of the churches, so that there will be no question in the minds of the members of any Church about the worth of the worship of any other Church. This recognition should also be popular, that is, the members of all churches, clerical and lay, should acknowledge and respect the value of the worship of every Church and feel free to participate in it.

Acceptance should extend to the many forms of worship as legitimate expressions of faith as the act by which we trust in Jesus and of faith as what we affirm in trusting in Jesus. (For further clarification of this distinction and its implications, see Section II on the unity we seek in belief. That section also offers grounds for the possibility of this recognition.)

Authentic Christian worship presupposes "the reality of ministry and priesthood of Word and sacraments as having their source in the Spirit and the risen Lord."[25] Lack of mutual recognition of this reality by the churches vis-à-vis one another has been and continues to be a major source of separation in worship. For these reasons, official and popular recognition should extend to the many forms of worship as grounded in mutually recognized ministries. For the possibility of this mutual acceptance, see the statement "Ministry in the Church" of this consultation,[26] also *Reconsiderations* by this consultation,[27] and Kilian McDonnell's "Ways of Validating Ministry."[28]

The many forms of worship should be recognized as instruments of God's saving action, in contrast to the centuries-long doubt, suspicion, and even denial of the efficacy of various Christian churches' worship. The possibility of this recognition is demonstrated by its partial realization, for example, among the various churches in the Presbyterian-Reformed tradition, and in Vatican II's statement: "The brethren divided from us also carry out many of the sacred actions of the Christian religion. Undoubtedly, in ways that vary according to the conditions of each church or community, these actions can truly engender a life of grace, and can be rightly described as capable of providing access to the community of salvation."[29]

A current obstacle to worship together is the sense of obligation which Christians feel to participate in their own denomination's worship. This feeling may arise from respect for the legislation of one's Church, from loyalty to one's own Church, or from suspicion of other churches' worship. In the unity we seek in worship, this narrow sense of obligation should no longer exist because the churches should recognize officially and popularly the many forms of Christian worship as satisfying obligations and expectations which may arise from belonging to one or another denomination. The possibility of this recognition lies in the previous acknowledgments and in a new understanding of the Church which cuts through denominational divisions and is articulated in this statement's Section I on the unity we seek in the Church as the people of God.

The many qualifying forms of worship should be recognized as fulfillments of personal and ecumenical needs. Thus, in good conscience, members of a denomination may choose the worship they will participate in on a given day. Because a person needs a supporting community for his or her Christian life and has actually become a member of a particular Church, he or she should usually share in that Church's worship. But because he or she needs to celebrate with a relative on the occasion of the latter's wedding, he or she may participate fully in the worship of another community on that day.

The possibility of this kind of recognition is manifested in the acknowledgment by many churches of the right of their members to participate in the worship of other churches as they see fit. Even the Roman Catholic Church, generally reserved in this matter, permits and even encourages its members to participate, under certain conditions, in the worship of Eastern Orthodox churches to satisfy a variety of personal needs.[30]

2. *New communities of worship.* The worship in the unity we seek should sometimes be celebrated, not by denominational congregations, but by groups of Christians from several denominations who experience together in a special way Christian proclamation (*kerygma*), service (*diakonia*), and fellowship (*koinonia*) and desire to express and nourish this experience in worship. These communities will be more associational than familial in character, that is, based upon conscious choice of specific objectives by the members rather than upon kinship, friendship, or intimacy, although the impetus of Christian love will open them to and perhaps even lead them to friendship and intimacy.[31] Obviously these groups will not be territorial parishes of any particular denomination.

The possibility of such communities flows from the recognition of a plurality of forms of worship which we have just described, and from what is proposed about the people of God, unity in belief, and cooperative organization in other sections of this statement.

3. *Active participation.* For a developed explanation of this feature, see the exploratory paper, "Toward the Unity We Seek in Worship," prepared for this consultation.[32] Here it is sufficient to point out that this active participation extends beyond the actual celebration of worship to include both planning the manner in which received forms of worship are celebrated and creating new forms of worship which meet the criteria of authentic Christian worship. Participation to this extent, involving laity as well as clergy, women as well as men, young and old, and other groups hitherto excluded from a say in the form of their own worship, will result in forms of worship more clearly related to Christian life and mission in the world, and more expressive of the equality of all in Christ, regardless of sex, race, ethnic background, and social or ecclesiastical status.

The possibility of such participation is evident in the steps which various churches have taken in recent years in this direction, in accord with growing awareness of the Church as the people of God, all members sharing in some way in the priesthood of Jesus.

4. *Integrity of Christian worship.* Naturally we expect the worship we seek in unity to possess those qualities which will make it authentically Christian and effective for Christian life and mission. Thus the worship we seek should be characterized not only by active participation of all but also by a combination of structure and freedom, an involvement of the whole person, a sense of transcendence, an orientation to mission, a balance of Word and sacraments, and a shared understanding of Christian worship. These characteristics are explained in detail in the paper "Toward the Unity We Seek in Worship" mentioned in no. 3, above, on active participation.

Steps Toward Unity in Worship

Evidence of the need for the kind of worship just described can be found in the local scene, as this consultation found it in Columbus, Ohio.[33] Responsible steps should be taken, therefore, to advance our respective churches toward such unity in worship. Such steps should be encouraged by those entrusted with leadership positions.

The Eucharist, or Lord's Supper, continues to be a vexing problem in our relationship. Presbyterian-Reformed and Roman Catholic Christians are often experiencing profound unity in marriages, in theological schools, in spiritual retreats, in cooperative action for social justice. Yet they are suffering because they are prevented from sealing their common Christian experience, witness, and mission by sharing in one another's Holy Communion or a common ecumenical one. The situation begets frustration, anger, and—it should be faced—disregard for Church discipline behind closed doors. Presbyterian-Reformed Christians feel insulted by Roman Catholic suspicion of the authenticity and integrity of their Reformed Holy Communion; Roman Catholic Christians fear that Reformed eucharistic doctrine underplays important themes and that, consequently, Reformed discipline is too liberal in its admission to the Lord's Supper and too casual in its treatment of the elements used in the celebration. These festering feelings of insult and of fear threaten to poison ecumenical relations.

Clearly, steps must be taken to clarify misunderstandings, resolve genuine disagreements, and move toward shared Eucharists. Toward this end, we wish to indicate first our agreement in regard to the Lord's Supper, then note differences, and finally make some recommendations in regard to both Holy Communion and other forms of worship.

We Roman Catholic and Presbyterian-Reformed Christians profess in faith that the Eucharist is the sacramental meal which Christ has given to his disciples. It is the effective sign of Christ's gift of himself as the Bread of Life through his offering of his life and death and through his resurrection. It is the great thanksgiving to the Father for all that he has done in creation and redemption, for all that he does today in the Church and the world, and for all that he will accomplish in the consummation of his reign. In the Eucharist the Church celebrates the unrepeatable sacrifice of Christ and shares in its saving power.

Christ instituted the Eucharist as the memorial (*anamnesis*) of his whole life, especially his death and resurrection. Christ himself, with all he accomplished for us and all creation, is present in this memorial, which is also a foretaste of his coming reign. This memorial, in which Christ acts upon his Church through its joyful celebration, implies this presence and anticipation. It is not merely a mental or spiritual recollection of a past event or its significance, but the proclamation-making-present the whole of God's great work in Christ Jesus, enabling the Church through its fellowship with Christ to share in that reality.

As the Church carries out this memorial of the suffering, death, and exaltation of Christ, our high priest and intercessor, we receive from the Father the fruits of the unique and perfect sacrifice of his Son and beg the Father to apply its saving power to every human being. Thus, united with our Lord who offers himself to the Father, and in union with the universal Church in heaven and on earth, we renew and offer ourselves in a living and holy sacrifice, which we must express also in our daily lives.

The memorial of Christ is the content of the preached Word as it is of Holy Communion. The celebration of the Eucharist supposes the preaching of the Word, for the Eucharist is meaningless without faith, and the preaching of the Word is the call to faith.

On the other hand, the Lord's Supper completes the preaching of the Word. The preaching of the Word is not merely an occasional service of the Church but pertains to its very nature as sent by the Lord; similarly the Eucharist is not merely a convenient service provided by the Church for individuals, but belongs to and manifests the very nature of the Church as a participant in the mystery of Christ.

This memorial, in its fullest sense, includes the invocation of the Spirit (*epiclesis*). Christ in his heavenly intercession asks the Father to send his Spirit upon his children. The Spirit, called upon the assembly and upon the bread and wine, makes Christ really present for us, gives him to us, and enables us to discern him. The memorial and invocation find their fulfillment in partaking of Holy Communion.

In the Eucharist the Lord himself says: "Take and eat; this is my body which will be given up for you. Take and drink; this is the cup of my blood of the new covenant which shall be shed for many for the forgiveness of sin." We profess, therefore, the real, living, active presence of Christ in this sacrament.

The discernment of the body and blood of Christ requires faith. The real presence of Christ in the Eucharist, however, does not depend upon the belief of each individual, but on the power of Christ's Word mentioned above and upon his promise to bind himself to the sacramental event as the sign of his person given to us.[34]

In this consultation's study of ministry in the Church, we reached agreement that "each church's ministry had been real long before members of the other church or churches came to admit it, indeed not withstanding its denial for centuries. Our respective ministries derive their efficacy from the presence of Jesus Christ, who is operative in them through his Spirit, and not from the recognition accorded by other Christian communities. . . . We cannot but recognize the risen Christ present and at work for the healing of his people in the ministry and Eucharist of each of our traditions."[35] We deemed it "a grace to have come to the realization that Christ is operative, however differently, in the ministries of both churches, and further ask that this realization be publicly recognized."[36]

We are united in affirming in faith the mystery of Christ's

real presence in the Lord's Supper in virtue of his Word and the power of the Holy Spirit. We diverge, however, when we begin to articulate this faith, as the following paragraphs illustrate.

On both sides, the real presence of Christ is affirmed in the assembled community, in the community's praise and thanksgiving, in the proclamation of the Word, in the speaking of the words of institution in the name, authority, and power of Christ, and in the partaking of the bread and wine.

But there are different ways of expressing Christ's presence in relation to the elements. Presbyterian-Reformed Christians prefer to speak of Christ's giving himself with the bread and wine. Roman Catholics say that through the conversion of the bread and wine Christ is really present under the appearances of bread and wine. These expressions reflect different appropriations of "how" Christ is present in relation to one factor in the total eucharistic event; they do not indicate a difference about the fact of his real presence in the total event. The different expressions have, however, resulted in different liturgical practices and attitudes toward the elements. The doctrinal implications of these differences should be explored.

This difference, which along with others provoked considerable discussion in this recent phase of our consultation, illustrates that in regard to the Eucharist much still remains to be clarified and, in some cases, to be worked through from disagreement to accord. Our differences and questions may reveal divergence in the articulation of faith rather than in faith itself. But in practice that distinction is not easy to observe; different articulations of faith may indicate different faiths by which people are actually living. Moreover, the distinction can be abused: people can worship together and yet hold different views difficult to reconcile, so that the witness to unity by worship is betrayed by disunity in everything from doctrine to moral decisions. We found this phenomenon occurring even within our denominations.[37]

Recommendations

We conclude with several recommendations that will promote the unity we seek in worship.

1. *Dialogue on the Eucharist.* We recommend dialogue on the Lord's Supper between our respective churches to resolve the

many questions which still exist about one another's celebration of the sacrament and generally hinder shared Eucharists. Members of our churches in a variety of ecummenical endeavors or on special occasions, such as weddings, desire strongly to share Holy Communion but are unable to do so for a variety of reasons, some doctrinal, some disciplinary, some attitudinal. This inability to share Holy Communion prevents participation together in full Christian worship, namely, worship through Word *and* Eucharist. It hinders our missionary witness to Jesus Christ as the one in whom humanity is united.

If the Roman Catholic Church still has doubts about the authenticity of the Lord's Supper in the Presbyterian-Reformed churches, then the Roman Church should immediately, humbly, with open mind, and in dialogue with brothers and sisters in Christ, examine the texts of Presbyterian and Reformed eucharistic liturgies, resolving the doubts or indicating precisely what is wanting.

Likewise, doubts which remain in many Presbyterian-Reformed circles regarding Roman Catholic teaching and practice should be honestly examined. It should be determined if in fact there are grounds for the fears that non-scriptural speculations have been raised to the status of dogmas and that the veneration of the saints, especially the Blessed Virgin Mary, has detracted from the unique honor of Christ. The actual teaching of the Roman Catholic Church, especially since Vatican Council II, and the devotional tradition associated with the Mass need understanding among Protestants.

2. *Re-education in teaching about the Eucharist.* We recommend comprehensive re-education of the members—lay and clerical—of our respective churches in regard to the Lord's Supper. Generally the eucharistic faith of the majority of the members of our churches does not possess the balance and fullness of eucharistic understanding which has emerged in scholarly study in recent decades. Many Christians have simple, clear-cut but overly simplistic faith in the Eucharist, focused on the "real presence of Christ" narrowly conceived and on the question whether it is or is not a sacrifice, with little appreciation of the ultimate reality, or grace, signified and intended by the sacrament. Many other Christians have such vague ideas about Holy Communion that one may

wonder if their faith really embraces the Eucharist. Neither of our communions can boast of the integrity and fullness of the eucharistic faith of its members. Nothing will be accomplished on the pastoral level in terms of eventual shared Eucharists if our churches settle for consensus on the Lord's Supper among an elite of scholars in dialogue and do very little to re-educate the laity and clergy at large.

3. *Occasional shared Eucharists.* We recommend occasional shared Eucharists for members of our churches. We reiterate our proposal adopted in our statement "Ministry in the Church":

> It must be faced, as we have seen, that serious divisions remain between Roman Catholic and Reformed Christians, divisions serious enough to preclude *general* eucharistic sharing for the present. Nevertheless, since we have moved significantly toward a greater recognition of each other's ministry and a common eucharistic faith, we believe that our churches should act not only with a consciousness of their own distinct identity, but also with a practical recognition of the common bonds already uniting them with one another. They should designate specific occasions on which invitations may be offered to celebrate together in the Eucharist the unity of faith which we have found in common and should provide effective means of striving toward the greater ecclesial union yet to be achieved. We therefore recommend to the ecclesiastical authorities to whom we are responsible the implementation of such *limited* eucharistic sharing.[38]

As a sign of unity, the Lord's Supper presupposes loyalty to Christ which, in practice, requires agreement on faith and order. But as this consultation notes elsewhere in this statement, the point at which differences in the articulation of faith become essential differences in faith itself is not always clear. In the case of Holy Communion, moreover, we are faced with a mystery attained only by faith and never exhaustively grasped in our frail human concepts and words. Before judging another's eucharistic faith inadequate, we ought to be mindful of our own limitations before this mystery of God's love.

We do have much in common as a basis for shared Eucharist. We have one baptism which makes us brothers and sisters in the one body of Christ, who is our common Lord and whom we both regard as the Lord who presides over our Eucharists. Together we are members of the one people of God in the new covenant founded upon and sealed by the one sacrifice of Christ efficaciously proclaimed, we both believe, in our Eucharists. We confess together the faith expressed in the Apostles' Creed and in the Nicene Creed, and we do not inquire beyond these creeds from communicants in our own churches when they approach the Table of the Lord. We profess together the eucharistic faith enunciated at the beginning of this section on the Eucharist.

The purpose of Holy Communion is to build up the body of Christ, to effect as well as signify the unity of the Church. Presbyterian-Reformed churches have communion open to all baptized believers in Jesus Christ as Lord and Savior, provided they are repentant.[39] Within the Roman Catholic Church, exceptions to the principle that the Eucharist is a sign of unity are already made for Protestants to share in the Catholic Eucharist on the basis that the Eucharist is also a source of nourishing grace for baptized individuals on their way to personal salvation.[40] Exception can be made as well on the basis that the Eucharist is a source of unifying grace for the divided pilgrim Church on its journey toward oneness in Christ.[41]

Even though differences remain to be resolved, sufficient grounds exist for occasional shared Eucharists, most especially where Roman Catholic and Presbyterian-Reformed Christians have discussed, or have been instructed about, the extent as well as the limitations of accord in regard to the Eucharist and about the meaning and implications of such shared Eucharists.

4. *Congregations' covenanting worship together.* In Section III of this statement, covenanting between congregations of our respective churches is explained. Here we wish to note that a particularly suitable and important matter for covenant agreements is worship. Roman Catholic parishes on the one side and, on the other, Presbyterian-Reformed congregations may covenant to have: representatives from each side attend the Sunday worship of the other once a month, even though this may exclude reception of Holy Communion for the present; joint services of worship on

special days, for example, on the Fourth of July and Thanksgiving in the civil year, on Pentecost and the First Sunday of Advent in the ecclesiastical year, on special occasions such as weddings and ordinations, and during the Week of Prayer for Christian Unity; joint study groups to learn more about one another's values, spirit, and traditions of worship; informal prayer groups; observers from the partner congregation at meetings of the session or parish committee concerned with worship; instruction of children about one another's worship in Sunday school, parochial school, and religious education programs. This list is only illustrative of possibilities.

5. *Education in one another's worship.* Religious educational materials (books, audio-visuals), curricula, programs, and actual instructions prepared in our respective churches, whether by local, regional, or national agencies or by individuals, should include instruction on each other's worship. This applies for all levels of education, namely, for children, youth, and adults. It is especially crucial for the education of those preparing for public ministry in the Church as ordained ministers or priests, religious educators, social workers, and so forth. Responsibility for taking initiative in this ecumenical education rests upon individual pastors, teachers, heads of schools or regional programs, as well as upon official local, regional, and national agencies. Publishers of educational materials can exercise great influence by requiring inclusion of such content in materials they publish.

6. *A Year of Ecumenical Worship.* Our respective churches could commit themselves, covenant, to sponsor a Year of Ecumenical Worship in 1980. Another year is possible provided it allows time for preparation. During this year our churches would cooperate in making known to one another and learning from one another our different heritages of Christian worship in the unity we seek. Sermon and homily aids could be jointly prepared to assist preachers in our churches on this theme. Agencies devoted to preparing religious instruction materials and religious publishing houses could be asked to develop the theme in their publications. Local congregations of our respective churches could enter into covenants, as described above, for the year. Roman Catholic bishops could encourage their people to fulfill their canonical Sunday obligation on special occasions by attendance at worship in Pres-

byterian-Reformed churches. Presbyterian-Reformed pastors could encourage their people to attend Roman Catholic worship on special occasions. Centers of liturgical study in both our communions could be asked to devote their programs to exploring the possibilities of worship between churches of the Roman Catholic and Presbyterian-Reformed traditions. The North American Academy of Liturgy, the North American Academy of Ecumenists, the Liturgical Conference, the Federation of Diocesan Liturgical Commissions, the National Ecumenical Workshop, the Commission on Interim Eucharistic Fellowship of COCU, and the Theological Committee of the World Alliance of Reformed Churches, North American Area, could be asked to take up this theme at their annual national and regional meetings. During this year, jointly prepared and officially approved rites of baptism and marriage could be introduced for common use, especially in celebrations involving members of our denominations.

This list of activities for a Year of Ecumenical Worship seems necessary to pull people out of their denominational preoccupations and raise the level of everyone's consciousness with regard to the problems, possibilities, and imperatives of worship together. More modest proposals often fail to capture the imagination and break through inward-looking institutional routine.

Notes

1. "When an image is employed reflectively and critically to deepen one's understanding of reality, it becomes what today is called a 'model' " —Avery Dulles, *Models of the Church* (Garden City, N.Y.: Doubleday, 1974), p. 21.

2. Vatican Council II, *Dogmatic Constitution on the Church*, no. 9, in Walter M. Abbott, ed., *The Documents of Vatican II* (New York: Guild Press, 1966), p. 26. See also: Yves Congar, "The Church: The People of God," in E. Schillebeeckx, ed., *The Church and Mankind*, Concilium 1 (Glen Rock, N.J.: Paulist Press, 1965), pp. 11-37; Eugene Burke, "The Shape of the Unity We Seek," paper submitted to the Roman Catholic/Presbyterian-Reformed Consultation, May 30, 1973, Columbus, Ohio.

3. Cf. infra: "The Shape of the Unity We Seek," Eugene Burke, pp. 83-84.

4. 1 Cor. 13.

5. See: *The Interpreter's Bible*, X, pp. 149-214; *The Jerome Biblical Commentary*, 51:73-81.

6. Vatican Council II, *Dogmatic Constitution on the Church*, no. 13, in Abbott, *op. cit.*, pp. 3-32.

7. Cardinal Jan Willebrands, "Moving Toward a Typology of Churches," *Catholic Mind* 68 (April 1970):35-42. See also: ARC-DOC 1, (Washington, D.C., 1971), p. 39.

8. *Ibid.*, p. 41.

9. Arleon Kelley, "Community and Institutional Factors in the Shape of the Unity We Seek," no. 2.4.1, paper presented to the Roman Catholic/Presbyterian-Reformed Consultation, May 30, 1973, p. 12.

10. Walter Kaspar, "Der ekklesiologische Charakter der nichtkatholischen Kirchen," *Theologische Quartalschrift* 145 (1965):62.

11. At New Delhi in 1961 the World Council of Churches stated that it is "a fellowship of churches which confess the Lord Jesus Christ as God and Savior according to the Scriptures and therefore seek to fulfill together their common calling to the glory of one God, Father, Son, and Holy Spirit. Our message to you is that 'God was in Christ, reconciling the world to himself, not counting against men their transgressions, and has given us the message of reconciliation' (2 Cor. 5:19)." From "Message to Member Churches" by the Nairobi General Council of the World Alliance of Reformed Churches, printed in *God Reconciles and Makes Free*, Reports from Nairobi, (Geneva, August 1970), p. 41; W. Visser't Hooft, ed., *The New Delhi Report* (New York, 1962), p. 152.

12. "I am the truth" (John 14:6) and "The truth shall make you free" (John 8:32).

13. It should be noted here that both Protestant and Catholic Scripture scholars recognize that the New Testament itself is also the written form of several "traditions" of the beliefs, the faith statements, of several of the first Christian communities.

14. Vatican II's *Decree on Ecumenism* makes a similar point when speaking of Eastern and Western Christianity: "It is hardly surprising, then, if sometimes one tradition has come nearer than the other to an apt appreciation of certain aspects of a revealed mystery, or has expressed them in a clearer manner. As a result, these various theological formulations are often to be considered as complementary rather than conflicting" (no. 17, in Abbott, *op. cit.*, p. 360).

15. In no. 11 of chapter 2 of the *Decree on Ecumenism* from the Second Vatican Council it is stated: "When comparing doctrines, they should remember that in Catholic teaching there exists an order or 'hierarchy' of truths, since they vary in their relationship to the foundation of the Christian faith. Thus the way will be opened for this kind of fraternal rivalry to incite all to a deeper realization and a clearer expression of the unfathomable riches of Christ (cf. Eph. 3:8)" (in Abbott, *op. cit.*, p. 354).

16. Writing on repentance and forgiveness, Calvin states: "Now if it is true—a fact abundantly clear—that the whole of the Gospel is con-

tained under these two headings, repentance and forgiveness of sins, do we not see that the Lord freely justifies his own in order that he may at the same time restore them to true righteousness by sanctification of his Spirit? . . . Christ entered upon his preaching: 'The Kingdom of God has come near; repent, and believe in the Gospel' (Mk. 1:15)" (*Institutes* III, 3:19).

"The idea of the Kingdom of God, the sovereignty of God, was a conception which was central and basic to the message of Jesus. He emerged upon men with the message that the Kingdom was at hand (Mt. 4:17; Mk. 1:15). To preach the Kingdom was an obligation that was laid upon him (Lk. 4:4). It was with the message of the Kingdom that he went through the towns and the villages of Galilee (Lk. 8:1). The announcement of the Kingdom was the central element in the teaching of Jesus" (William Barclay, *The Mind of Jesus* [New York: Harper & Brothers, 1961], p. 47).

"Calvin was the only one of the original reformers to make a clear distinction between doctrinal articles concerning necessary elements of the faith and other articles concerning points of doctrine about which different opinions can be held without endangering the unity of the Church (*Inst.* IV.1:12). On this basis later Reformed theologians (Junius, Jurieu, Turrettini) developed the theory of the fundamental articles which were to serve as a sufficient foundation for the reunion of the Churches.

"This theory was worked out in such a rationalistic way that it did not find wide acceptance. But the underlying conception of a hierarchy of truths has slowly but surely made its way. It is reflected in the Basis of the World Council of Churches (where the fundamental articles have become the God-given Person). It has now even been recognized in the Roman Catholic Church. For the very first time an official Roman Catholic document has declared that there exists a hierarchy of truths since they vary in their relation to the foundation of the Christian faith (*De Ecumenismo* II, 11)" (W. Visser't Hooft, "Relevant Characteristics of the Reformed Position," *Bulletin of the Department of Theology of The World Alliance of Reformed Churches* 9, no. 4 [Summer 1969]:6-7).

17. For example, "Women in the Church," *Journal of Ecumenical Studies* 9 (1972):235-241; "Ministry in the Church," *ibid.*, pp. 589-612.

18. For example, "Most Important Statement Since Reformation for Anglicans and Catholics—Agreed Statement on Eucharistic Doctrine," *ibid.*, pp. 222-26; *Documents on Anglican/Roman Catholic Relations II* (United States Catholic Conference, Washington, D.C., 1973); *Lutherans and Catholics in Dialogue I-III*, ed. by Paul C. Empie and T. Austin Murphy (Augsburg Publishing House, Minneapolis, 1974); *Lutherans and Catholics in Dialogue IV* (Augsburg Publishing House, Minneapolis, n.d.); *Papal Primacy and the Universal Church*, ed. by Paul C. Empie and T. Austin Murphy (Augsburg Publishing House, Minneapolis, 1974); *Lutheran-Episcopal Dialogue* (FM Maxi Book, n.d.); *Modern Ecumenical Documents on the Ministry* (SPCK, London, 1975).

...

19. The 1647 edition of the Westminster Confession reads: "There is no other Head of the Church, but the Lord Jesus Christ: Nor can the Pope of Rome, in any sense, be head thereof: but is, that Antichrist, that Man of sin and Son of Perdition, that exalteth himself, in the Church, against Christ, and all that is called God." The present edition, adopted by the United Presbyterian Church in the United States of America in 1958, reads: "The Lord Jesus Christ is the only head of the Church, and the claim of any man to be the vicar of Christ and the head of the Church is unscriptural, without warrant in fact, and is a usurpation dishonoring to the Lord Jesus Christ" (*The Book of Confessions* [Philadelphia: Office of the General Assembly of the United Presbyterian Church in the United States of America, 1970], Chapter XXV, paragraph 6). The derogatory term "popish" is also dropped from the 1958 edition in Chapter XXII, paragraph 7, and Chapter XXIX, paragraph 2.

20. Vatican Council II, *Decree on Ecumenism,* no. 19, in Abbott, *op. cit.*, p. 361.

21. "Ministry in the Church," *Journal of Ecumenical Studies* 9 (1972):611-12.

22. *Ibid.*, p. 604.

23. The Pauline and Lucan accounts imply that a meal intervenes between the sharing of the bread and partaking of the cup, while the Marcan and Matthean accounts imply that the two acts have been brought together (cf. 1 Cor. 11:25; Lk. 22:20; Mk. 14:23; Mt. 26:27).

24. Chapters 12-14 of 1 Corinthians are devoted to the problems occasioned by spontaneous prayer in the gatherings of the Corinthian church.

25. "Ministry in the Church," no. 10, *Journal of Ecumenical Studies* 9 (1972):608.

26. See note 21, *ibid.*, pp. 589-612.

27. *Reconsiderations: Roman Catholic/Presbyterian and Reformed Theological Conversations 1966-67* (New York: World Horizons, Inc., 1967), pp. 122-37, 139-53.

28. *Journal of Ecumenical Studies* 7 (1970):209-65. See also Franz Josef van Beeck, "Towards an Ecumenical Understanding of the Sacraments," *Journal of Ecumenical Studies* 3 (1966):57-112.

29. *Decree on Ecumenism,* no. 3, in Abbott, *op. cit.*, p. 346.

30. Secretariat for Promoting Christian Unity, *Directory 1967*, nos. 44-50.

31. See Raymond H. Potvin, "The Religious Group as Community," paper presented to the Roman Catholic/Presbyterian-Reformed Consultation, May 9, 1974, Columbus, Ohio.

32. Meeting of October 24-26, 1974.

33. See papers prepared for this consultation at its meeting May 30-June 2, 1973, namely: Arleon L. Kelley, "Community and Institutional Factors in the Shape of the Unity We Seek: Sociological Input, Bi-Lateral Consultation, Columbus, Ohio"; Eugene M. Burke, "Report on Presby-

terian-Roman Catholic Task Force, Columbus, Ohio"; Sally Cunneen, "Report on Ecumenical Task Force Visit to Columbus, Ohio, Jan. 11-17."

34. As the basis for our discussion and statement regarding the Eucharist, this consultation used the agreement composed by a group of Reformed, Roman Catholic, and Lutheran theologians meeting at the Trappist Monastery in Les Dombes, France, September 6-9, 1971; see: "Accord doctrinal entre catholiques et protestantes sur l'Eucharistie," *Documentation catholique*, no. 1606 (April 2, 1972):334-38. In the short time allowed for our discussion of the Lord's Supper we were unable to reach mutual understanding on all the aspects of the Eucharist which the Europeans did, as comparison of our statement with theirs reveals. The eucharistic portions of this consultation's statement "Ministry in the Church" should not be overlooked, however. Other bilateral consultations in the United States, moreover, have reached significant agreement with regard to the Lord's Supper; see the Anglican-Roman Catholic Consultation, U.S.A., "Comment on the 'Agreed Statement on Eucharistic Doctrine' of the Anglican-Roman Catholic International Commission" (*Journal of Ecumenical Studies* 9 [1972]:690-91); also *Lutherans and Catholics in Dialogue, III: The Eucharist as Sacrifice* (1967) and *IV: Eucharist and Ministry* (1970).

35. "Ministry in the Church," no. 10, *Journal of Ecumenical Studies* 9 (1972):608.

36. *Ibid.*, p. 609.

37. ". . . it is a fact that within our respective churches members of the same communion often are drifting farther and farther apart, not living together at all, though they are frequently worshiping together" (no. 9, *ibid.*, p. 608).

38. No. 11, *ibid.*, p. 610, emphasis in original.

39. For example: "An invitation to partake shall be extended to all who confess their faith in Jesus Christ as Lord and Savior, and may include baptized children when their families deem it appropriate, if the session authorizes" (United Presbyterian Church in the U.S.A., *Directory for the Worship of God*, 21.04).

40. "As for common worship (*communicatio in sacris*) . . . it may not be regarded as a means to be used indiscriminately for the restoration of unity among Christians. Such worship depends chiefly on two principles: it should signify the unity of the Church; it should provide a sharing in the means of grace. The fact that it should signify unity generally rules out common worship. Yet the gaining of needed grace sometimes commends it" (Vatican Council II, *Decree on Ecumenism*, no. 8, in Abbott, *op. cit.*, p. 352).

For application of these principles in regard to Eastern churches and in regard to other churches and ecclesial communions, see Secretariat for Promoting Christian Unity, *Directory 1967*, nos. 38-65, and *Instruction Concerning Cases When Other Christians May Be Admitted to Eucharis-*

tic Communion in the Catholic Church, May 25, 1972, no. 4, where it is stated: "The *Directorium Oecumenicum* has already shown how we must safeguard simultaneously the integrity of ecclesial communion and the good of souls. Behind the *Directorium* lie two main governing ideas: (a) the strict relationship between the mystery of the Church and the mystery of the Eucharist can never be altered, whatever pastoral measures we may be led to take in given cases. Of its very nature celebration of the Eucharist signifies the fullness of profession' of faith and the fullness of ecclesial communion. This principle must not be obscured and must remain our guide in the field. (b) The principle will not be obscured if admission to Catholic eucharistic communion is confined to particular cases of those Christians who have a faith in the sacrament in conformity with that of the Church, who experience a serious spiritual need for the eucharistic sustenance, who for a prolonged period are unable to have recourse to a minister of their own community and who ask for the sacrament of their own accord. This spiritual need should be understood in the sense defined above (No. 3, b and c): a need for an increase in spiritual life, and a need for a deeper involvement in the mystery of the Church and of its unity."

41. "Yet though it is a spiritual food whose effect is to unite the Christian man to Jesus Christ, the Eucharist is far from being simply a means of satisfying exclusively personal aspirations, however lofty these may be. The union of the faithful with Christ, the head of the mystical body, brings about the union of the faithful themselves with each other. It is on their sharing of the eucharistic bread that St. Paul bases the union of all the faithful, 'Because there is one loaf' (1 Cor. 10:17). By this sacrament 'man is incorporated in Christ and united with his members.' By frequent receiving of the Eucharist the faithful are incorporated more and more in the body of Christ and share increasingly in the mystery of the Church" (Secretariat for Promoting Christian Unity, *Instruction*, May 25, 1972, no. 3, b).

Remarkable is the fact that Roman Catholic documents avoid, though they do not deny, application of the principle that the Eucharist is the cause of the grace which unites the Church as well as the expression of that grace of unity. In regard to the Eucharist as cause of grace, they apply that principle only in regard to the grace necessary for individuals' salvation, neither affirming nor denying explicitly its application in regard to the grace necessary to unify the Church.

Washington, D.C.
May 24, 1976

The Consultation

The Most Reverend Ernest L. Unterkoefler
Bishop of Charleston — Chairman

The Reverend Andrew Harsanyi, Ph.D. — Vice-Chairman

REFORMED

Dr. Paul J. Achtemeier
Dr. John W. Beardslee, III
The Reverend Mrs. Margrethe B. J. Brown
The Reverend Chalmers Coe, D.D.
The Reverend Raymond V. Kearns, Jr.
Dr. Violette Lindbeck
Dr. J. A. Ross Mackenzie
The Reverend Nathan VanderWerf
The Reverend William B. Ward
Dr. E. David Willis

ROMAN CATHOLIC

The Very Reverend Msgr. Henry Beck
The Reverend Schuyler Brown, S.J.
The Reverend Eugene Burke, C.S.P.
Mrs. Salley Cunneen
The Reverend Christopher Kiesling, O.P.
The Reverend Frank B. Norris, S.S.
The Reverend Raymond H. Potvin
The Reverend N. Robert Quirin
Dr. Leonard Swidler

SPECIAL CONSULTANT—NCC

The Reverend Arleon L. Kelley

BCEIA STAFF

The Reverend John F. Hotchkin
The Reverend J. Peter Sheehan

Part Two

BACKGROUND PAPERS

The Task Ahead—Some
Observations for Discussion

The purpose of this paper is to raise the kinds of questions and stimulate the kind of discussion that will get us started on this next round of meetings of the Roman Catholic/Presbyterian-Reformed Consultation. These random thoughts are presented without the least intention of being a set program for the next several years. It will become clear that the paper has not even raised all the *questions* which need to be raised as we begin this new round of talks. It will have served its purpose if it initiates the kind of discussion which enables us, by the end of these days together, to clarify and perhaps outline our program of work for this next series of meetings.

I think it is clear to all of us that the atmosphere in which we begin this round of talks is very different from what it was when the first round was begun, just after Vatican II. Ecumenical dialogue was then still a novelty, and the general mood was one of euphoria about Christian unity, an issue which could claim widespread public interest. At the same time there was a kind of vagueness about just where it would all lead; it was characteristic of that period that when questions were asked about the concrete shape of unity, the question would be deferred by an appeal to the unknown designs of God, who would somehow bring some kind of unity out of it all.

Today we are in a different world, and the movement toward Christian unity is neither novel nor widely popular. In his excellent article describing the new situation of ecumenism, Kilian McDonnell sums up the new factors in the situation:

> When the Gospel itself loses a clearly recognizable identity . . . because of the new spiritualism, linguistic skepticism, radical secularism, the evacuation of the numinous, the loss of particularity and social unrest, then both the church and the ecumenical movement lose plausibility (*Commonweal*, vol. 95, October 15, 1971, p. 58).

To these factors one could add others which touch more directly upon the inner politics of each of the churches, and pervading them all, like gray, oppressive smog, the mood of apathy which debilitates the movement at all levels.

If we take a backward look at what this consultation has done since it began shortly after the Council, we see that it, like the other bilaterals, directed its attention toward theological questions. Yet, unlike the other bilaterals, as far as I can make out, it did not confine itself to such issues. The division of the group into sections on Theology and on Worship and Mission provided for attention to more practical and concrete issues as well as those of a deeper theological kind, but it is not clear to me that the advantages of this division outweighed the disadvantages. I was not in the group from the beginning, and do not know how the decision was reached to proceed in this way. In retrospect, I am more aware of the limitations this procedure placed on the effectiveness of the group than of the ways it helped. As one who was heavily involved in the work of the Theology Section, I think I would have to confess, in all honesty, that the collection of papers and joint statements issued by, for instance, the Lutheran/Catholic bilateral group were superior to what we produced. I suspect the reasons for this, or at least some of the reasons, are that their group concentrated exclusively on the theological task, without dividing their energies, and that, from the beginning, they planned an orderly program of work. At the same time, it would be only fair to note that a number of concrete practical programs were carried out by the Worship and Mission Section, a kind of thing which, as far as I know, did not happen in the other bilaterals.

So where do we go from here? Let us first take a look at the program for this coming round of talks which was agreed upon at the concluding meeting of the last round, and then comment upon it:

> The focus of its work should be the concrete goal of the Christian unity of our Churches. Its first task would be, in on-going

dialogue, to describe as clearly as we can the shape of the unity our churches seek. The next task would be, on the basis of concrete study of the real situation of our churches in this country, to discover what concrete steps can be taken toward this goal. These steps would be a description not merely of what is already accepted by our churches in this country as possible, but of what new possibilities can be opened up by their mutual agreement, and particularly what the first such new step or steps would best be. The delineation of concrete steps would be set forth with awareness that as circumstances change, the nature and order of these steps might well need to be revised. Those chosen for this task should have the varieties of competence this task requires.

Why did the group choose this route? Different persons probably voted for this approach for different reasons, but here are two reasons which inclined me to favor this approach. First of all, considerable doctrinal agreement has been achieved, enough so that we should be able to begin to carry through with some concrete action toward unity. Secondly, the task of working toward doctrinal agreement is one in which others can engage and are engaged. The on-going theological enterprise in both of our churches continues along this line in a number of settings: seminary clusters, joint theological dialogue groups at all levels, and publication in journals, to name some of them. But this Consultation has a particular mandate over and above the general task of working toward better understanding and deeper agreement in theology. This Consultation, at least as I understand it, is officially commissioned by the churches which have constituted it to move the churches corporately toward the goal of Christian unity. This is a goal which presupposes the groundwork of theological dialogue, but goes a step further. It seems only right that this Consultation concentrate on the particular task it has to accomplish, a task to which no other group is commissioned in precisely the same way.

Beginning with the agreed program for this round of talks, what can we hope to achieve at this first meeting? Hopefully we will be able to outline a serious and specific program of work as well as agree on the amount of time we think proper to give to it and the frequency of the meetings over that designated time.

As we go about this task, it seems to me that there are four important things we need to do:

1. identify the shape of the unity we seek;
2. identify the kind of concrete things which should happen if this unity is to grow;

   3. identify the obstacles which stand in the way of reaching the unity
      we seek;
   4. identify precisely what *this* consultation can do to move us toward
      this unity.

   In all of this we need to be conscious that we are not talking of Christian unity in general or at random, but of the Roman Catholic and Presbyterian-Reformed Churches here in the United States in 1972, with all of their peculiarities and idiosyncrasies, weaknesses and strengths, as they exist on the national level, on the diocesan and presbytery level, on the parish or congregational level, and on the level of individual to individual.

   The rest of this paper will deal in order with the four above points.

The Shape of the Unity We Seek

   Perhaps the unity we seek could be described in general terms as that in which each church brings to this unity the variety and richness of its own tradition, yet the common structures, formulas of faith and joint actions come together more and more in such a way that the members of both churches will grow together with deeper unity in the Spirit. We might even say that the norm for determining the visible shape of unity could be: "What really contributes toward nourishing and deepening this communion in the Spirit? What really makes this communion effective in the task of bringing a share in this same communion to the world through healing and reconciliation?" I will not be more specific than that, because it seems to me that our main task now at the beginning is to be clear about the norms we are setting for determining the visible shape of unity. If we can do that, it will then be possible to picture to ourselves what the shape should be. Furthermore, while we should hope to be more concrete in describing the shape of the unity we seek between our churches than we were ten years ago, realism demands that we acknowledge that this picture can only become fully clear as we grow together in the coming years.

The Concrete Things That Will Make This Unity Grow

   A major fact to remember as we address ourselves to this practical problem is that unity is not a once-and-for-all either-or terminus that will (or will not) be achieved at a given moment in the future. This is true whether we are talking about the unity of all Christians or the unity of Roman Catholics and Presbyterian-Reformed, or the unity of either Roman Catholics or Presbyterian-Reformed among themselves. To a degree unity already exists; the task is one of deepening it and of strengthening all the links which build it. And these links are many and diverse. The fabric of unity is woven of many separate strands.

What are these strands? What are the elements of the unity of the Christian Church? One of the most obvious differences between the different kinds is that some are visible (structures, actions, doctrines) and some are in the hearts and minds of those united. It might be a practical way for us to proceed if we were to draw up as complete a list as possible on the bonds, visible and invisible, which constitute this unity. We might even then list them in the order of their practical attainability, or, better, ask ourselves which of them (because easier to obtain or because more pivotal in achieving the goal) a wise strategy would suggest we deal with most immediately and energetically.

This unity is a body-spirit thing. It is not simply the unity of pure spirits, but of men and women, body-persons, and to talk exclusively of spiritual, invisible unity is to disregard reality as it is. Nevertheless, it is true that what is central is the spiritual dimension, that communion of hearts and minds which is livened by the one Spirit. Indeed, this communion is a precious value in itself, quite apart from whatever else accompanies it. One of the reasons why many Christians show little sympathy for the ecumenism of top-level dialogue or of merger is probably that they have the conviction that this inner communion in the Spirit of which we have been speaking is the principal goal which the externals of the Churches are meant to serve. In this they are perfectly correct. What they often seem to overlook, however, is that spiritual unity cannot exist in a vacuum. It is only through a visible web of interconnections that this spiritual unity can come to birth, be nourished and sustained, and grow. Yet if we are to take their objections seriously, the changes and links we make in the visible structures and actions of our churches must be those which will truly deepen that spiritual communion which is the most important thing of all. It is quite possible that the new structures and actions which will at present be most effective in deepening this communion will be those which fail to exist not because of some existing Church law or doctrinal difference, but because of sheer apathy and smug self-content in living within the comfortable boundaries of one's own congregation. A regular series of joint dinners for two neighboring Catholic and Presbyterian parishes, for instance, which would not infringe the existing regulations of either of the churches in the slightest way, might well do as much to deepen their real community in Christ as a couple of instances of eucharistic sharing, which at this stage would go counter to the existing regulations as they are normally interpreted by Church officials.

I am becoming more and more convinced that it is above all in sharing together at the local level that Christians must grow together. The main importance of breakthroughs and agreements at higher levels is to release and stimulate forces at the place where they become most significant, at the local level where the lives of Catholics and Presbyterians can meet and where the spiritual community they already share in a partial way can grow deeper and richer.

Here is an initial, pump-priming list, thrown together in the order in which they came into my head, of elements which make up the complex web of the unity we share and need to deepen:

1. the unity of being physically present together at the same time in the same place;

2. the unity of actually having the same attitude toward life, a shared set of beliefs, even where there is no meeting or sharing beyond that (the kind of unity which supposedly a California Roman Catholic has with a German Roman Catholic he has never met, or a Pennsylvania Presbyterian has with a member of the French Reformed Church);

3. the unity of joining together to achieve some purpose, which can be on many levels, for instance:

    a. to make the Gospel of Jesus Christ known and shared;

    b. to perform any of the "corporal works of mercy";

    c. to perform any of the "spiritual works of mercy";

    d. to bring about peace in the world;

    e. to bring about justice for the oppressed (à la SODEPAX);

4. the unity of praying together;

5. the unity of celebrating the same ritual together;

6. the unity of singing the same hymns, even though in separate places at separate times (common hymnal);

7. the unity of using the same prayers or formulas of worship, even though in separate places and at separate times;

8. the unity of agreement on what is morally right and wrong;

9. the unity of possessing money or property in common (whatever happened to St. Mark's in Kansas City?);

10. unity of common places of theological education to train for the ministry;

11. unity of shared experiences of "retreats";

12. unity of more fully shared celebration of marriage ("mixed" marriages);

13. unity of the life of prayer and witness of couples in "mixed" marriages;

14. unified set of policies for celebration of "mixed" marriages (e.g., that it should be celebrated in the church of the bride with the clergyman of her church officiating);

15. common Bible-study courses jointly sponsored by Catholic and Presbyterian-Reformed congregations or larger groups;

16. joint programs for the Christian education of children;

17. the unity of sharing differences; what I have in mind is some kind of a gathering at which the differences which divide Catholics from each other and which also divide Presbyterian-Reformed from each other (such things as can be briefly indicated with such words as conservatives vs. liberals) could be dealt with together.

This is not even the beginning of a complete list, and perhaps it is even unbalanced in the partial summary it gives, but it should give some idea of what I mean and prime the pump for further additions to make the list more complete and balanced.

The Obstacles

One way of looking at the task of building unity is to consider the positive elements that constitute it. That is what we have just been doing. Another way is to draw up a list of the obstacles that hinder the strengthening of unity. Here is a sample list to get us started:

1. apathy and inertia;

2. separate ownership of churches and property;

3. separate organizations of officials, staff organization, all of what makes up a separate institution;

4. the existence of almost totally separate networks of interrelations, one Catholic, the other Presbyterian-Reformed (at this point I think we have to admit honestly the existence within each of the two churches, within each of these two separate networks which barely intersect, the divisions of separate worlds within each of the churches; unity is not just a task between the separated churches, but within each of them as well);

5. concern of the Roman Catholic Church at the top official level for unity with the Eastern Orthodox Churches, which tends to discourage moves which could be obstacles to Roman Catholic/Orthodox unity (such as Catholic approval of the idea of intercommunion, a sensitive issue with the Orthodox) but which could be aids to Catholic/Presbyterian-Reformed unity;

6. concern of Presbyterian-Reformed in the United States to give first priority to unifying the Presbyterian-Reformed family, leaving less energy to devote to the task of Roman Catholic/Presbyterian-Reformed unity;

7. difference of numbers (at the local level, for instance, in some cities there might be six Catholic churches and two Presbyterian ones, which makes for a difficult relationship);

8. different teachings in the areas of marriage, divorce, abortion and sexual morality generally;

9. conviction of many individuals on both sides that religion is just a matter of each individual's personal relation to God;

10. the growing disinterest, especially of younger people, in involvement in the life of the churches, which can have the effect of turning the attention of pastors and congregations toward the problem of their own institutional survival, and away from the larger, more outgoing issues of unity with other Christians (although this may not be the only or the most reasonable reaction to the phenomenon, it is not hard to understand).

What This Consultation Can Do

Once again, here is a list of sample possibilities to get our discussion started:

1. induce the churches in this country at the official level to establish new concrete policies together which will be more conducive to unity, and which will liberate and stimulate those at the local level;

2. take concrete means to remove obstacles and establish structures at the local level to strengthen unity;

3. prepare a handbook of concrete things that can be done at the local level by Roman Catholic and Presbyterian-Reformed congregations and their pastors to strengthen unity;

4. set up a traveling team of facilitators (composed of Roman Catholic and Presbyterian-Reformed members) who will go to the local scene and activate a concrete program to bring about actions and structures that will strengthen unity;

5. encourage the setting up of some joint national projects with Catholics and Presbyterian-Reformed (open, of course, to other churches who might want to take part) to tackle concrete problems where the Christian task of healing and reconciliation can be accomplished (sample issues: prison reform, war and peace, violence in our society, genetic engineering);

6. above all, it would seem important to establish some joint structures that would work steadily over the coming years to deepen unity, especially at the local level. As an example of the importance of this point, let me point to two instances within my experience at the Graduate Theological Union in Berkeley. The courses at all the schools are open to any student from any of the schools, and the schools are physically close enough to each other so that attendance at these classes is easy. The result is that practically every class has a good mixture of students from the different schools—Catholic, Presbyterian, Anglican, Lutheran, etc. This structure goes on working every day to strengthen the Christian unity of the men and women who are in these classes together. On the other hand, there are no established structures for shared worship. There have been, over the years, a few scattered examples of shared worship of one kind or

another, but there is no on-going pattern to give constancy to this element of unity. I mention this example to stress the importance of establishing on-going structures which bring Roman Catholics and Presbyterian-Reformed together. Without them, how can they ever really come to a significantly stronger Christian unity?

These observations have been patchy and incomplete, but, given the purpose of this paper, that may not be a bad thing. After all, it is not intended to serve as a completed outline of our task for the next several years, but only as an opener to get the discussion started.

Yet I do hope that it will be possible, before these few days together are over, to get the goal of this next round of talks clearly focused and agreed on in our minds, and to outline a clear and serious program of work for ourselves.

Daniel J. O'Hanlon

The Shape of the Unity We Seek

Introduction

This paper is oriented in terms of the general thematic this consultation has chosen: The Shape of the Unity We Seek. It is developed here specifically in the light of the study group's experience in Columbus, and the reflection and discussions that went on there and subsequently. Added to this is a considerable body of reading and personal reflection arising out of this experience and our reaction to it. As a result I have come to see three principal considerations that constitute the horizon and the thrust of this paper.

1. At this point in our ecumenical dialogue I have become convinced that we must enlarge their scope if we are to have a horizon worthy of our primary purpose—unity. Up to this point our conversations have been interdenominational and the bilateral groupings have been in denominational terms. Thus the Roman Catholic/Presbyterian-Reformed consultation is by its grouping a denominational discussion. While I believe the structural approach was not only necessary but valuable, it seems to me now that it has been a foundational first stage. Once you turn your thinking to the shape of the unity we seek, then a much more extensive and vertical vision is called for. Obviously this does not imply that we can now ig-

nore the denominational lines of demarcation, for they represent the factual realities that ecumenism must fully account for or be ultimately destined to interesting but meaningless dialogue. For while the unity of the Church is a "given" of the Christian faith, it does not exclude a plurality of local churches. Yet this unity is not seen as compatible with a number of conflicting denominations that often reject the legitimacy of doctrine and ministry in other groups. In fact while contrary to the ideal held out in the New Testament, such divisions are a continuing element of the history of the Christian Church. So we are called to oneness but divided in fact. Hence the effort here is to try to see these factual divisions, recognizing them as a divisive element in our dialogue. Yet at the same time must we not envelop them in a much larger context of theological perspectives that we can share in common? These perspectives, however, will be of no value if they portray unity in terms of the lowest common denominator. Rather the purpose of this paper is to flesh out what I consider common positive elements of our Christian theological tradition and some of the consequences that flow from them.

2. Looking back on the experience of the past seven years and the time left to us in our present program, I have chosen to use this paper to bring to your consideration a long-range proposal that need not necessarily end with the conclusion of the next two years. This proposal consists in formulating an organic program ordered to our purpose and theme and able to be employed and continued in cooperation with the other consultations. It would seek to be a second stage in our endeavor to envisage the shape of future unity. Thus the considerations advanced in this paper are not intended to be imposed on or restrictive of our future discussions. They seek to formulate a somewhat detailed set of subjects as a suggestion whereby we might set for ourselves an ordered process in which we endeavor to concretize our chosen thematic.

3. While I have been thinking of these first two presuppositions (or perhaps classically "prolegomena") a third one has come to the fore in these past few months. Derived from the contribution made to our task force by Dr. Arleon Kelly, it is the necessary role that the sociology of religion must play as we attempt to project the future. Purely theoretical theological speculation, while exciting, has no ultimate effectiveness unless it is grounded in the actualities of man in his existential condition. Unless "religion be understood as a human projection grounded in specific infrastructures of human history any theological project will tend to be rootless," for we will have failed to take into full account the socio-historical presumptions that in a very special way are characteristic of the Judaeo-Christian religious tradition (e.g., its radical historical orientation as lin-

ear rather than cyclic). "Only after the theologian has confronted the historical relativity of religion (the character of religion as a human product) can he genuinely ask where in this history it may be possible to speak of discoveries, i.e., that transcend the relative character of their infra-structures." (Cf. Peter Berger, *The Sacred Canopy*, Appendix II, "Sociological and Theological Perspectives," pp. 180-185.)

It is with these ideas in mind brought out by Dr. Kelly that the study group decided to present two general papers for your consideration—one theological and the other from the standpoint of the sociology of religion. Dr. Kelly and myself have discussed in considerable detail the correlation of these two papers, and while no effort has been made to force a programmed dovetailing, still we believe that they will be mutually complementary.

I

A. *Ecclesiology*

(In this whole approach I should like to call special attention to J. Robert Nelson's article "Toward an Ecumenical Ecclesiology" in *Theological Studies*, Vol. 31 [1970], pp. 644-673.)

I begin here with the theology of the Church because any effort to describe future unity must begin with some kind of model of what we mean by Church. Concretely, as indicated above, the Church, and the churches, set our problematic. In developing this ecclesiological approach, I have elected to begin with scriptural sources and biblical theology, and so I have selected three thematics: the Church as a building and as being built; the Church as the people of God; the Church as the body of Christ.

1. *The Church as a Building and as Being Built.* This notion of building and building up has a rich and multi-faceted biblical history. Here I am particularly concerned with the Pauline usage in 1 Corinthians and again in Ephesians. The treatment in 1 Corinthians 3:9-17 is not directly ecclesiological but has implications of it. For it is clear that St. Paul sees the conflict of parties in Corinth as a threat to the unity of the Church, and he seeks to mediate it. Apollo and Paul are both servants but it is God who sets up and maintains the whole building. However, Paul has laid the foundation (v. 11) and no other foundation can be laid in the place of it. Thus each must take care how he builds on it, for the first and permanent foundation is Jesus Christ. It is this foundation that is laid by Paul's preaching. The Gospel of Christ preached by St. Paul is both the Gospel

concerning Christ and the Gospel in which Christ proclaims himself. Thus there can be no other foundation because no other Gospel can be preached save that preached by St. Paul.

In Ephesians 2:20-22 the image emphasizes primarily the universal Church and so is directly ecclesiological, for here it is the second generation of Christians that are addressed—the Gentiles as fellow heirs and members of the same body. Here the foundation is "the apostles and the prophets" (a general term for the first generation of Christian teachers through whom the Church has moved from Judah to universality of outlook. But Christ is the cornerstone who joins the foundation with the building and gives both their shape. He is the norm for the apostles and prophets, and the Church grows out of this because the whole structure is joined together through Christ. (Cf. F. Schnider and W. Stenger, "The Church as a Building and the Building Up of the Church," *Concilium*, Vol. 80 [1972], *Office and Ministry in the Church*, pp. 21-34.)

In the Pauline usage, the notion of building up which he employs in a number of places underlines the spiritual task of the believing community in the history of salvation. This task is an on-going reality involving growth and development. It is a dynamic image. This becomes clear in Ephesians 4:11-16. Christ is the permanent foundation of the Church and its cornerstone, but the Church itself is never perfect. It is the Church becoming and never at its goal. "The Church is the eschatological community not in itself, but only in and through its relationship with Jesus Christ. . . . This building is still growing and is never complete within time." But growth means that a distinction can be made between what is fixed and what is changeable. What is fixed is the eschatological foundation of Jesus Christ and its universal spread through the apostolic Church (*ibid.* p. 34).

2. *The Church as the People of God.* This biblical image, as applied to the Church, is given contemporary currency by Vatican II. In the course of the debates, the effort to describe the Church as a whole shifts from the notion of mystical body to the notion of the people of God. Ultimately this theological development becomes Chapter II of the *Constitution on the Church*. It is set between Chapter I on the mystery of the Church and Chapter III which treats of the hierarchy, and particularly the bishops. The whole chapter intends to explain how the Church develops itself in human history, how this Church expands and reaches out to various categories of men unequally or divergently situated with regard to the fullness of Christ and what all the members of the people of God have in common in their Christian existence. (I have chosen to take this section of the *Constitution on the Church* because it attempts to set forth a working

synthesis of common ecclesiology, for a primary consideration in both the debate and final formulation is an abiding ecumenical concern. Finally this chapter itself responds to a deeply felt need to go beyond the merely juridical and sets the Church in the whole plan of salvation. Therefore, its emphasis is on the historical dimensions of revelation and thus on the human and communal side of the Church. Cf. "Symposium on 'People of God,' " *Theology Today,* vol. XXIX (April 1972) pp. 22-53, especially Michael Despland, "A Theological Appraisal," pp. 34-45.

The idea of the people of God has deep biblical roots in the Old Testament. Here it means first of all that Israel is the people of God, since in its experience of faith (exodus and covenant) it owes its national religious existence to God and his historical action. This basic affirmation is quite closely related to the notion of God's assembly (the Ecclesia), i.e., the people of God assembled before the Lord in covenant and law. At Vatican II, more than twenty years of biblical and theological reflection converge into this second chapter. The Old Testament presents an affirmation of the people of God as a religious society chosen by God for his service. It is at the same time an earthly society united by race, language, country and civil laws. Yet it is prophetically understood as imperfect and awaiting a new universal covenant in the future. (Cf. X. Leon-Dufour, S.J., *Dictionary of Biblical Theology*, p. 368-374. Also P.S. Minear, *Images of the Church in the New Testament*, especially chapter 3.)

It was out of this that exegetes and theologians began to rethink the Church's understanding of itself and see its relation to the doctrine of the mystical body that had dominated Catholic teaching since Pius XII's encyclical on the subject. It was Canon Cerfaux who showed that the conception of the Church as the body of Christ was neither central nor fundamental to St. Paul's definition of the Church. Cerfaux insisted that St. Paul began with the Old Testament notion of Israel as the people of God, for it is Israel as a people that has given the covenant and the promises, the worship of the true God, and his presence. Therefore their assembly is called the Church of God, so that the fundamental notion of Christ's Church is the People of God. St. Paul, however, sees Christians as a new people linked with Israel and therefore also an Ecclesia. But the profound unity of the various communities (churches) with Christ as well as the heavenly dimension of the Church in Christ brings St. Paul to describe the Church in the Spirit as the body of Christ. It is a dimension or attribute that brings out the transcendent element of the Church. (Cf. L. Cerfaux, *La Theologie de l'Eglise suivant Saint Paul* (1948), "La theologie du Pueple de Dieu," pp. 3-111 [I have here used this edition to evidence the early development before Vatican II]. Cf. also Frank B. Norris, *God's Own People: An Introductory Study on the Church*.)

Since Cerfaux's treatment there has been further development. The doctrine of the body of Christ is not simply an attribute but an essential concept of the Church. "The Church is the New Testament people of God, founded by Jesus Christ, hierarchically structured, ministering to the advance of God's Kingdom and the salvation of men, and this is the mystical body of Christ." (Cf. M. Schmaus, *Katholische Dogmatic*, Vol. III, p. 48.) Congar sees St. Paul's introduction of the idea of the body of Christ as an essential concept in order to explain what the people of God had become since the incarnation, Easter, and Pentecost. (Cf. "The Church: The People of God" in *Concilium*, Vol. 1, pp. 36-37. This whole essay is a summary of the thinking that led up to Vatican II and gives an extensive bibliography. Cf. also Karl Rahner, "People of God," *Sacramentum Mundi*, 400-402.)

3. *The People of God in the Theology of Vatican II.* I have chosen to take this section on the *Constitution on the Church* because I believe that it attempts to set out a working synthesis of our common theological tradition on the Church. The whole chapter on the people of God finds its fundamental thesis set forth in the opening section, no. 9. (Cf. *The Documents of Vatican II*, ed. W. Abbott, p. 24.) It is the affirmation that the coming of salvation calls for the establishment of a community of salvation. Unquestionably each man's decision is personal as it must be before God in Christ and his Spirit. Yet it is also clear that God's saving action in history is directed to the formation of a community of salvation. It must be noted though that this community looks to perfect fulfillment only at the end of time. In human history God proceeds by gradual stages, as shown in the election, covenant, and guidance of Israel. Thus this national entity, with its specific human and social and cultural characteristics, constitutes the first stage. Yet prophetically it reached out to all humanity. The new covenant in Christ, however, places this community of salvation on a new basis. For now with Christ, the fullness of revelation and the inner personal relation to the salvation are set in a new community of salvation. This community is not based on natural descent or a common nationality, but on a new covenant inaugurated in the blood of Christ, marked by acceptance of God's Word in faith, and sealed by baptism. Thus the individual's participation makes him a member of a new people, the community of the baptized "as a fellowship of life, charity, and truth" (*ibid.*, p. 26).

Emphasis must be laid on the significance of the new Israel, the new community of Christ, which is the Church. Ultimately it is by the will of God that the community of salvation is called, gathered by his grace, and so constituted. Its historical cause is Christ who offers salvation, unity, and peace, and it is man's free assent to these that serves to constitute the visible community. Implied in this is the acceptance of the unity of mankind to be brought about by this community of salvation—the people of God. "God has gathered together as one all those who in faith look upon Jesus as the author of salvation and the source of unity and peace, and has established them as the Church, that for each and all she may be the visible sacrament of this saving unity" (*ibid.*). As with the Old Testament, the recipient of salvation, the vessel of God's mercy, is primarily the people. Thus the universality of the people, the Church as partner in the covenant, and the individual as a member of the promised people all make clear that the paths of God's salvific work lead to the community. Recognized in this section are the tensions that beset the Church historically and geographically, in space and time, through the weakness of the flesh. But "moved by the Holy Spirit she may never cease to renew herself, until through the cross she arrives at the light which knows no setting" (*ibid.*).

4. *Sociological Implications.* The sociological implications of this theological exigency of a "community of salvation" are the professional concern of Dr. Kelly. Yet speaking from a religious or, perhaps more accurately, a para-theological point of view, I should like to introduce some considerations that have struck me. As our other papers indicated, the question of the Church as a community was very much a part of the experience and concern expressed to us. Since then my own approach has been further developed by the last volume of *Concilium*, Vol. 81, *The Persistence of Religion*. The editorial that introduces this volume, written by Andrew Greeley, articulates a point that I have only vaguely verbalized. He asserts:

> The function of this issue is not to persuade theologians that religion persists as to point out the multiplicity and complexity of religious persistence. The sacred and the secular, the religious and the profane, are not opposite poles of an evolutionary model but alternative dimensions of reality which interrelate with one another and interpenetrate one another in complex periodicity ["periodicity" would refer to alternating rhythms such as Church and sect] (p. 7 and p. 34).

In the course of his own article, "The Persistence of Community," Father Greeley quotes at length from R. Nesbit's *The Sociological Tradition:*

> By community I mean something that goes far beyond mere local community. The word as we find it in much 19th and 20th century thought encompasses all forms of relationship which are

characterized by a high degree of personal intimacy, emotional
depth, moral commitment, social cohesion and continuity in
time. Community is founded on man conceived in his wholeness
rather than in one or another of the roles, taken separately, that
he may hold in the social order (pp. 47-48).

Father Greeley would hold that however accurately this describes the past,
today there is frequently a new dimension. This dimension is one of inter-
personal intimacy characterized by a powerful and systematic trust (*art.
cit.* pp. 24-25). He, of course, recognizes the dangers in this but here simply states a fact. It is this fact that, looked at theologically and seen
together with Nesbit's definition, seems to me to call for some treatment
here.

First, as the *Pastoral Constitution on the Church in the Modern
World* affirms, today a growing number are aware of themselves as ar-
tisans and creators of the culture of their community and so there is
growth in the combined sense of independence and responsibility. It is this
general move toward awareness of personhood and self as a responsible
agent that is central to this development. "This truth grows clearer if we
consider how the world is becoming unified and how we have the duty to
build a better world based upon truth and justice. Thus we are witnesses of
the birth of a new humanism, one in which man is defined first of all by
his responsibility toward his brothers and toward history." (Cf. Abbott,
op. cit., p. 261.)

Gregory Baum, commenting on this solidarity and common destiny,
insists that it cannot be reduced to purely moral terms: it must include
faith and hope. "For men are profoundly touched not only by the conviction that human life is not as it ought to be, but also by the unaccountable
faith that human life is meant to be different, that it is up to us, to people,
to transform it and that by doing so we follow our call and destiny." He
sees this experience as having a dimension that is specifically religious.
"For man's vocation is not man-made. Man encounters his destiny; he
discovers it, he receives it, is addressed by it, marvels at it, and makes it
the ground of his hope." Baum sees this new religious experience as profoundly affecting the lives of the churches and leading Christians to understand the message and call of Jesus in a new way quite in harmony with
valid aspects of the Christian tradition. (Cf. *Concilium,* Vol. 81, "The
Survival of the Sacred," pp. 20-21.)

5. *The Prophetic Office of the People of God.* The *Constitution on
the Church* brings out the participation of the people of God in Christ's
kingly rule, his priesthood, and concludes that this people by reason of

redemption is a priestly people. However, here I have chosen to select an area that more directly affects our ecumenical ecclesiology and pastoral renewal, for Article 12 of the Constitution (Abbott, pp. 29-30) describes the fullness of the Christian life as seen in Christ's prophetic office. As a mediator of the fullness of revelation, as the bearer of all the messianic gifts through the Spirit, Christ shares with his people both his mission and his fullness. For Christ as the true witness of God's Word conveys the realities of revelation and its saving gift to be the living possession of his people—his body. Now in the *Constitution on the Church*, two points are stressed—the indefectibility of the people of God, and the charisms that are given to the people of God. With regard to the first, indefectibility, two things may be pointed out. First, the Council does not treat of the question of ecclesial infallibility (or indefectibility in faith) in any fullness. Its concern is a specifically Roman Catholic one and does not look directly to the ecumenical dialogue. From this point of view it speaks of "the supernatural sense of the faith that characterizes the people as a whole." It manifests therefore "this unerring quality . . . from the bishops to the last member of the laity [when] it shows universal agreement in matters of faith and morals." Of particular importance here is that what is involved is the working of the Spirit in the entire people. Whatever of indefectibility may be found in the hierarchy has its roots in this fact and not vice versa. Secondly, emphasis is needed to insist that this sense of the faithful is not a source of revelation nor does it constitute revelation. As the Theological Commission explained to the Council, it is a kind of faculty belonging to the whole Church by which the Church sees in faith the revelation which has been transmitted, discerning the true from the false in matters of faith, and at the same time penetrating more deeply into it and more fully applying it to its life. (Cf. Abbott, *op. cit.*, p. 46.)

More important for the moment for our ecumenical concerns is the whole matter of charisms. This role of charisms in the life of the Church is, I believe, quite crucial in our ecumenical development. The importance of charisms for ecumenical issues is to be seen in the fact that they are an integral part of the Pauline ecclesiology. It is easy and in fact has been a dominant attitude that the hierarchical structure of the Church appears as an administrative apparatus with no intimate connection with the charismatic gifts of the Spirit which are spread through the life of the Church. (Cf. Suenens, *Council Speeches of Vatican II*, ed. by H. Küng, Y. Congar, D. O'Hanlon, p. 29.) While St. Paul recognizes extraordinary signs, the true charism looks to service. Thus it serves the community in a responsible way. These gifts look to the renewal and building up of the Church, and these in turn are directed to the more excellent way—charity. Thus the "charismata are not primarily extraordinary but common; they are not of one kind but manifold; they are not limited to a special group of persons but truly universal in the Church. All this implies they are not only a thing of the past (possible and real only in the early Church) but eminently contemporary and actual; they do not hover on the periphery of the Church but are eminently central and essential to it. In this sense one should speak of the charismatic structure of the Church which embraces and goes beyond the government of the Church." (Cf. Hans Küng, "The Charismatic Structure of the Church," *Concilium*, Vol. 4, p. 58; also K. Rahner, *The Dynamic Element in the Church*, 42-82; Gabriel Murphy, *Charisms and Church Renewal*, pp. 93-140.)

Cardinal Suenens in his *Co-Responsibility in the Church* balances this whole approach very well:

> Certainly without the ministry of the pastors the charisms of the Church would be aberrant. But on the other hand, without these charisms the ecclesiastical ministry would be impoverished and sterile. It pertains to the pastors of the local churches or the pastor of the universal Church to discern these charisms of the Spirit by a spiritual intuition and to nourish and increase them.

> It pertains to the pastors of the Church to listen carefully and with open hearts to the lay people who so often enter into dialogue with them, and are endowed with their own gifts and charisms and often have a greater experience of the life of the world today (pp. 217-218).

Certainly, it seems to me that the understanding of charism presented in the preceding paragraphs make it possible to understand both the ecumenical movement as a whole and the individuals who have participated in it and do so now. As Hans Küng says: "Charism so understood does not mean an enthusiasm that supports the arbitrary or mere uniformity but the order in liberty that is the sign of the charismatic Church. 'Where the spirit of the Lord is there is freedom' (2 Cor. 3:17)" (*art. cit.*, p. 61).

B. *The Theology of the Local Church*

In introducing this material on the local church it is my conviction that we are dealing with a central element in any theologizing about the shape of the unity we seek. To conceive of an organic union that rises above all denominational structures, or tries to ignore them, is to chase after a will-o'-the-wisp. Such a conception simply ignores the historical situations and the realities of man's experience. More than this, it raises up objections across the board from conservatives to radical progressives that befog the ecumenical search. What it does is seek a kind of unification that makes our call to union in love a basic ecclesiological model as though distinctions and diversities will evanesce. John Haughey, S.J., treating this in *America* (April 1973, "The Fog Around Ecumenism") feels that "mergering" as a medium to union is a blind alley. Rather he would think that the ancient notion of *communion* is the true model for ecclesiological unity. "Communion, at a very minimum, involves a recognition and respect for one another as well as reverence for the distinctiveness of one another and a mutual desire for communication. What is presumed of the entity entering into communion is a sufficiently stable identity so that the process itself is enriching rather than something that could erode its individuality or internal cohesiveness." As Father Haughey views it in the ancient Church, "Difference and oneness was of the very nature of the Church. Of its essence it was and is a *corpus ecclesiarum*, a body of churches."

In the article noted in the preceding paragraph, Father Haughey makes reference to a lecture by Cardinal Willebrands that is quite crucial to the matter but which has not received in the United States the attention that it deserves. The lecture, entitled "Moving Toward a Typology of Churches," delivered in Great St. Mary's Church, Cambridge, England, on January 18, 1970, and reprinted in *The Catholic Mind* (April 1970, pp. 35-42). In the course of his address he treats of the ecumenical dialogue up to that date (1970). Then he asks whether it would be courage or rashness to offer some further perspective, some patterns perhaps, for the future. He invites his listeners to reflect on what theologians have been fruitfully discussing: "It is that of *typos* in its sense of general form or character and of a plurality of *typoi* within the communion of the one and only Church of Christ" (*art. cit.*, p. 40). In this he intends to go beyond the theology of the local church as it is found in Vatican II. Here what the Council was emphasizing was that the local church was not simply a part of the whole but that the fullness of the whole universal Church is present in the local church. (Cf. *Decree on the Bishops' Pastoral Office in the Church*, Abbott, *op. cit.*, pp. 396-429.)

While seeing this as important, Cardinal Willebrands desires to elucidate a distinct notion which he calls *typos*. This notion "does not primarily designate a diocese or a national church (although in some cases it may more or less coincide with a national church). It is a notion which has its own phenomenological aspects with their particular theological meaning" (*art. cit.*, p. 40). Therefore "where there is a long coherent tradition commanding men's love and loyalty, creating and sustaining a harmonious and organic whole of complementary elements, each of which supports and strengthens the other, you have the reality of a *typos*" (*ibid.*, p. 41). Such a *typos* would have "a characteristic theological method, e.g., historical rather than metaphysically structured; a characteristic liturgical expression: this expression would be engendered by its own psychology and its own experience of the divine mystery, e.g., sober and restrained or splendid and exuberant; a spiritual and devotional tradition, that is, a confluence of many streams: biblical, patristic, monastic, active, contemplative; a characteristic canonical discipline derived from both psychology and experience. This is borne out by the *Constitution on the Church*: "Various churches established in diverse places by the apostles and their successors have in the course of time coalesced into several groups, organically united, which, preserving the unity of faith and the unique divine constitution of the universal Church, enjoy their own discipline, their own litturgical usage, and their own theological and spiritual heritage." (Cf Abbott, *op. cit.*, p. 46.)

Article 13 of the *Constitution on the Church* gives special attention to this matter of the local church under the traditional term "catholicity." While many of the polemical approaches to catholicity on the part of the Roman Catholic Church centered on the geographical unity, this hardly did justice to its deeper meaning. The problem was further intensified by the term "Roman Catholic Church." Here the term "Catholic" was being used in an exclusive sense. (Cf. "The Meaning of Catholicity," *The Ecumenical Review*, 16 [1963-64], pp. 24-42. This article consists of three parts: the Preface by Dr. Lucas Vischer and the reproduction of two addresses given at the Fourth World Conference on Faith and Order [1963] by Vitaly Borovoy and Claude Welch.)

In the final version of the *Constitution on the Church* what is explicitated is that all members of the one people of God throughout the nations are in *communion* with one another. At this point this communion refers only to Roman Catholics in communion with the See of Rome. I believe, however, that the principle has a wider perspective and will treat it in this paper under the heading "The Church and the Churches." In general, catholicity is envisaged as a union of opposites. On the one hand there is the people of God in its unity and unicity (uniqueness) engraced by the Spirit. The other pole of this axis derives from the multiplicity of the peoples of the earth joined with the variety of customs, talents and energies. Insofar as these produce genuine values they can be employed to bring into the family of Christ all those who are called to the one people of God. So the gifts of the Spirit and the natural endowments of the people enable the people to form a local Church with its own way of living the Christian life. (Cf. Aloys Grillmeier in *Commentary on the Documents of Vatican II* [ed. H. Vogrimler], footnote on p. 167.) (N.B. Perhaps it is necessary to note that this element does not exclude universality or the need to bring all the riches of humanity back to Christ its head in the unity of the Holy Spirit.)

The other aspect of the local church I should like to treat here is the ancient usage, revived at Vatican II, termed "collegiality." As a term it leaves a good deal to be desired, but it has sufficient currency to let it ride here. My concern as noted is the local church, and for practical purposes I am using the Catholic administrative model of diocese or region. As a model here it is only intended to be illustrative, not normative. (Its application to a particular parish or congregation is still very spotty and on the whole excessively dependent on the local pastor.) For the early Church the term "Ecclesia" meant primarily the local church. Thus the Church is actualized in the individual local church. These local churches are not seen as simply on-the-spot administrative agencies or units; rather, each encompasses the total reality which is "the Church." Thus each local church is a living cell, and each cell contains the total living mystery of the one body which is the Church.

Each of these local churches has a vertical structure in the ancient usage, i.e., they are united in the bishop. (N.B. Again let me insist that this is a model and not as such a doctrinal affirmation. All it does is express a vertical dimension present in Scripture as "overseeship.") However, while the local church is a totality containing fully the essence of the Church, it is also open—in communion with the other church. This is also a necessary element of the local church—a kind of horizontal element whereby the catholicity of the local church is achieved through its communion so that by maintaining "overseeship" apostolicity is kept in focus. It is what we may describe as the "principle of episcopacy." (Cf. J. Ratzinger, "Pastoral Implications of Episcopal Collegiality," *Concilium*, Vol. 1, pp. 43-50.)

Collegiality, emphasizing the principle of episcopacy, makes the bishop a servant of the local church—his communio. Contemporary theology has seen this service as a building of community. Today community in the interpersonal sense would appear to be a Christian exigency, and this means a developing sense of co-responsibility. It is this understanding that has called for and in many cases evoked priests' senates, diocesan and parish councils and a discussion of a national pastoral council as well as planning for regional councils. The results have been uneven and in many cases it has been a slow learning process (not to say an extensive re-education). However, they do exist and I am hopeful at the growing assurance of a number of priests' senates in some larger dioceses. Of particular interest to the Catholic is the growing awareness that lay persons must be integrated as fully as possible into this co-responsibility shared on every level. Again the results are uneven and scattered (but for someone like myself the most important thing is that it exists at all). Here again the ideal is a real interaction of the horizontal and vertical, between the people of God in the local church and their leadership—the vertical element. (N.B. This vertical element I have left for other discussions because it seems to me that what I have called the horizontal movement—communion and communities—is where we are and where we should start.

Problematics Concerning the Local Church. Let me begin here with the Roman Catholic problematic. Over the past hundred years a combination of what were seen as organizational and theological demands plus the rapidity of communication has given a powerful and pervasive thrust to centralization in the Roman Catholic Church. Much of this is understandable in its age, but today there is a growing counter-thrust toward decentralization and the recognition of pluralism. Much of the polarization in the Roman Catholic Church focuses on this. For what this centralization has in fact done is to make the local churches administrative appendages.

The best treatment of this type of administrative processes I have seen is in a paper delivered to the Catholic Theological Society this past year by Mr. John Noonan, entitled "Making One's Own Act the Act of Another's." In treating the general theme of Church law and the humanization of man, Mr. Noonan selects among several categories what he terms "agency." By agency in this context a free person acts at the direction of another without great discretion and so makes his act count as the act of others. Thus such legal concepts as delegation, proxy, and agency and such things as power of attorney have become quite crucial to our Western culture. Recognizing that agency is a necessity for large communities, commercial corporations and government itself permit men to organize their activities, extend their power and build their communities in multiple ways beyond the boundary that would hold if persons had to relate to each other in person. It is this last point that is ecclesiologically important here. Agency is acceptable where what is done does not seem to require any special personal quality. "In the general run of cases where persons are aiding each other, the use of an intermediary means a loss of knowledge, in love, in reciprocal recognition of humanity." (Cf. *Proceedings of the Catholic Theological Society*, Vol. 27 [1972], pp. 32-44.) The whole system of agency and delegation tends to depersonalization and develops a kind of tutorial immaturity in decision-making. (It may be of help here to note that small fast-growth corporations have seen the necessity of shifting to this personal emphasis. Executive personnel is handled not through organizational charts but through the resources of the behavioral sciences to insure genuine, personal participation and concern.)

Relevant here may well be the principle of subsidiarity introduced into Catholic social thought by Pius XI in his encyclical *Quadragesimo Anno* as against the omnicompetent state. "It is a fundamental principle of social philosophy . . . that people should not withdraw from individuals and commit to the community what they can accomplish by their own industry and enterprise. So too it is an injustice and at the same time a grave evil and a disturbance of right order to transfer to the larger and higher collectivity what can be performed and provided for by lesser and subordinate bodies" (n. 79). This same principle of subsidiarity is explicitly repeated by John XXIII in his *Mater et Magistra* (n. 53).

The Protestant Problematic. The first thing to recognize here is that the roots of the Protestant problem are historically conditioned vis-à-vis the Roman Catholic Church. For the Reformation the whole stress on centralization from Avignon through the sixteenth century was to be equated with papal absolutism. Much of Luther's effectiveness lies in the consciousness he gave to the distinct witness of the German nation and its response to God's Word. Not only popularly but throughout the society of his time, the Roman Curia is the symbol of complacent disinterest for the German needs. To be noted also is the fact that Reform Protestantism as a whole was profoundly anti-papal. It is this characteristic that is the most general and the most striking of all the Reformation characteristics. Without question it belongs to all the fractions of Protestantism. It establishes among them all an unarguable kinship. They can and do differ on many things, but they do not differ in this regard whether it be Luther or Calvin or Zwingli or Cranmer or their disciples. (Cf. L. Cristiani, "Reforme," *Dictionnaire de Theologia Catholique*, Vol. 13, Part 2, cols. 2028-2029.) I include this historical issue in this paper because it colors not only our talking about the local church but also our overall concern with unity. It must not be lost sight of, for the whole thing has deep psychic and even unconscious roots that a relatively few years of general ecumenical dialogue have far from excised. My own opinion is that this also works against attempts to develop a clear-cut vertical dimension for the local church in American Protestantism.

Denominationalism. This of course is a fact of American life in particular and tends to differ sharply from the European confessionalism. Denominationalism is not a simple phenomenon but a complex one whose local and regional dimensions must be given full attention in any effort at ecumenical generalization. As Dr. Kelly has pointed out in his Columbus Report, denominationalism can be and is an impediment. It can readily involve "misconstrued priorities" whereby "the denomination is first, the

Church second." Thus, as he expresses it: "There seems to be a very great feeling of 'we' and 'they' "—"we" being a denomination, "they" being the ecumenical appendage. The result is that while in ecumenical conversation they may be affirmative, yet in the denominational councils those affirmations are not implemented. In view of this, Dr. Kelly writes: "The apparent generalization is that the larger the numerical base of the denomination in a given area, the more difficult they are to work with on an ecumenical basis." Certainly this leads to a careful and sometimes negative reaction to any positive kind of larger overseeship. There can be a very jealous concern with local prerogatives which may well be justified in the light of particular experience.

A further element is described by Dr. Martin Marty in his *Righteous Empire*. He points out that frequently a foreign visitor will expect that the denominations that have given shape to Protestantism will serve to define its basic divisions. But it is not this simple. What separates is not necessarily doctrinal positions at all. Rather the more fundamental divisions which Dr. Marty sees as crossing denominational lines are what he calls "private Protestantism" and "public Protestantism." Private Protestantism (which also assumes the title "evangelical") accentuates "individual salvation out of the world, personal moral life congruent with this ideal, and fulfillment in the rewards of the life to come" (p. 179). Public Protestantism (social) concerns itself with the social order and the social destinies of man. It strives to transform the world. Its concerns are not revival and the stimulation of conversion, but emphasis on the Kingdom of heaven on earth (*ibid.*).

It is in the light of this type of division that, as long as the national offices or international groupings confine themselves to purely informational and intra-church operations, there is no basic complaint. But if the aims of public and social gospel are given priority, then frequently uneasiness, doubts, resentment and ultimately opposition on the part of the local and regional churches develop. (This same situation is very much a part of the polarization that has taken place in the Roman Catholic Church since Vatican II on precisely the large social issues of war and peace, violence, racism, and poverty. The polite terminology is conservative vs. progressive; the more emotional description is reactionary vs. radical, and from there on the descriptions tend to degenerate.)

The Church and the Churches. Under this heading we must seek to deal with one of the most difficult areas in any kind of ecumenical ecclesiology. As already indicated, the unity of the Church in Christ is a revealed vocation. Yet it is equally clear that divisions of every kind are the ordinary history of the Christian Church. How then is it possible to understand the facts in such wise that we can honestly think of a common ecclesiology?

First, it appears to me that in the scene of the Reformation/Counter-Reformation world created during the last four hundred years, one of the central points that must be dealt with is the theological position developed in the Roman Catholic Church during this period. It is what Father Avery Dulles describes as the "substantialist approach." (Cf. "The Church, the Churches, the Catholic Church," *Theological Studies*, Vol. 33, pp. 199-234.) Writing in 1955, Gustave Thils sums up this position: Christ founded a Church. This Church is one, holy, catholic, and apostolic, and thus a visible and historical communion. It is to this communion that is given the assurance of indefectibility. It has existed *quoad substantiam* from its foundation until now and so to the end of the world. (*Histoire doctrinal de mouvement occumenique* [1955], p. 170) Therefore he criticizes the World Council of Churches for defending "a concept of the Church according to which the true Church of Christ does not exist *quoad substantiam* in a determinate historical community" (*ibid.* p. 173). This is to be described as the "exclusivist" position whereby all other "churches" can be called churches only in the sociological descriptive sense. Thus from the nineteenth century into the 1950's the Roman Church deals with non-Catholics only as individuals and never as members of a Church. The ultimate expression of this is by Pius XII in his *Mystici Corporis*, which affirms that the Roman Catholic Church and the mystical body of Christ are one and the same thing. Since the 1950's, this inflexible approach has been counterpointed by another, though unofficial, position. While asserting that the Church of Christ exists perfectly in the Roman Catholic Church, still it is found imperfectly or by participation in the existence of vestigia and gifts in other churches. (Cf. G. Thils, *op. cit.* [revised, 1963], pp. 142-147.)

At Vatican II there was a real effort to construct a broader vision of the Church and the churches. Tentative but determined, this effort does confront the past approach, yet it cannot wipe out the past or ignore its strong support by many members of the Council. As I would see it, therefore, the positions taken at Vatican II represent a stage in the self-understanding of the Roman Catholic Church as it reflects on itself in the light of the ecumenical movement. This is borne out by such statements as: "The greatest merit of the Constitution is that, far from canonizing the past, or even consecrating the present, it prepares for the future." (Cf. G. Dejaifve, "La 'Magna Charta' de Vatican II," *Nouvelle revue theologique,* Vol. 87 [1965], p. 21.) Similarly Bishop Butler declares: "I have no hesitation in saying that the Constitution is a great document even though, being the fruit of the Holy Spirit working in imperfect human

beings, it is a stepping stone and not a final accomplishment." (Foreword
to Paulist Press edition of *The Constitution on the Church*, Deus Books
[1965], pp. 8-9.)

Some of the steps taken at Vatican II in the development of this stage
need to be noted. First, the "exclusivist" approach of Pius XII in his encyclical *Mystici Corporis* is replaced by a fundamentally different one.
(Cf. G. Baum, "The Ecclesial Reality of the Other Churches," *Concilium*,
Vol. 4, pp. 68-70.) The Council teaches that the body of Christ and the
Catholic Church are not simply identical but diverse aspects of the same
complex reality. These aspects are not the same in the existential and historical order. Thus there is no necessary co-extension between the transcendent community of grace and the social body of the Church. In whatever way they are joined they may have historically distinct dimensions.
Vatican II sees the Church of Christ as transcending Roman Catholicism,
and the *relator* at Vatican II, in explaining the change here from "est" to
"subsitit," states that it was made "so that the expression may harmonize
better with the affirmation concerning the ecclesial elements that are present elsewhere," i.e., the ecclesial elements of sanctification and truth that
can be found outside the Catholic Church. This usage of "subsitit" is quite
important here. For "est" would have indicated an exclusive judgment of
identity and so excluded the other Churches from the concept of Church
(even analogically). Some of the Council Fathers called for this, or at least
for "subsitit in integro modo." The Theological Commission, however,
maintained "subsitit in" and so deliberately left open the question of the
relation of the one Church to the many churches. "A development of un-
foreseeable dimensions was thus made possible." (Cf. Aloys Grillmeier,
"The Mystery of the Church," *Commentary on the Documents of Vatican
II* [ed. H. Vorgrimler], p. 150, footnote 29.) Finally there is a shift from a
long-standing formulation of membership in the Church as either real or
by desire. What is presented instead is the notion of degrees of participation. At first glance this does not seem to be much, but in fact it represents a shift from a substantial exclusivist position and opens new horizons for Catholics in ecumenical dialogue.

This stage of Vatican II ecclesiology must also take into account the
Decree on Ecumenism where there are specified points touched only in
principle in the *Constitution on the Church*. The first note struck in the
Decree states: "Some, even very many, of the most significant elements or
endowments which together go to build up and give life to the Church herself can exist outside the visible boundaries of the Catholic Church." (Cf.
Abbott, *op. cit.*, n. 3, p. 345.) Since these communities have by no means
been deprived of significance and importance in the mystery of salvation,
the preaching and sacramental ministry "can truly engender a life of

grace, and can rightly be described as capable of providing access to the community of salvation" (*ibid.*, p. 346). In employing the terminology "churches and ecclesial communities" the Council left open its application. However, since the Council was acting on an ecclesiology that calls for the seven sacraments and an apostolic ministry transmitted through an unbroken series of episcopal ordinations, the implication is that ecclesial communities designate those bodies which "because of the lack of the sacrament of orders . . . have not preserved the genuine and total reality of the Eucharistic mystery" (*ibid.*, n. 22, p. 364). To appreciate the thrust of this position there must be adduced what I would see as another stage in the whole matter. This is the bilateral consultations (on the national and international level) that have centered on ministry. Out of this has come a more flexible attitude toward ministry and apostolic succession which we will see further on in this paper. (Cf. *Lutherans and Catholics in Dialogue*, Vol. IV, *Eucharist and Ministry* [1970]: "Presbyterian/Reformed-Roman Catholic Consultation"; "Statement on Ministry," *Journal of Ecumenical Studies* [Summer 1972], pp. 589-612. To this should be added the very considerable body of periodical literature on the Church ministry, its history and its development. It was this question of priesthood, episcopacy, and papacy, and what should be the Protestant response to it that troubled a number of observers at the end of Vatican II. Cf. V. Vajta, "Priest and Laymen," *Challenge and Response: A Protestant Perspective of the Vatican Council*; F. W. Katzenbach, "Some Consequences of Conciliar Ecclesiology," *ibid.*, pp. 207-210.)

The whole purport of this section on the Church and the churches is the eschatological dimension which is integral to ecclesiology. The import of this is synthesized by Walter Kasper: "Far more important is a fundamentally new theological overview of the relationship between the Church and the churches, a view that no longer treats this relationship purely statically and juridically, but dynamically and in the perspectives of salvation history. The unity and catholicity of the Church are always *in fieri*; they will always remain a task. The solution cannot lie either in mutual absorption or in a simple integration of individual ecclesiastical communities but only in the constant conversion of all, i.e., in the readiness to let the event of unity, already anticipated in grace and sign, occur again and again in obedience to the one Gospel as the final norm in and over the Church." (Quoted by Avery Dulles, *art. cit.*, p. 230, from "Der ecclesiologische Character der nichtkatholischen kirchen," *Theologische Quartalschrift*, Vol. 145, p. 62.)

Consultation on Church Unity. Because this issue arose in a number of contexts during the study in Columbus, it is treated here for the sake of completeness. Even more so, it is illustrative of better than a decade of joint effort to construct a model for organic union. For many this effort appears to have ended in practical failure; for others it has acquired the status of a kind of theory that needs to be assimilated and grown into. For still others, conservative, radical, charismatic (all have entirely different reasons), it has been and is opposed totally. These groups agree in rejecting it as well as any effort at what is termed· "organic union." Some of these have seen this proposal as ecclesiastical triumphalism, or an effort to create a monolithic structure or a power seeking denominational maneuver.

However, I believe that it has been an extremely important stage in the effort to concretize ecumenical unity. For if we are ever to escape endless discussions with no concrete commitment, some sort of model of organic unity must be envisaged. As a model it need not be universally applicable but at least it should be able to offer options that are specific enough to evoke commitment or rejection. In all of this the plan of union proposed by C.O.C.U. still has a good deal to offer; both what it states and the experience of those who support it and those who reject it should be a permanent part of any on-going discussion of the shape of unity we seek.

The problems raised by C.O.C.U. and other similar efforts is evaluated in an excellent article by the Reverend J. W. Grant (a professor of Church history in the Toronto School of Theology and Chairman of the Committee revising the Canadian plan of union) entitled "Church Union and the Up-to-Date Ecumenist" [*The Ecumenist,* Vol. 10, Sept.-Oct. 1972], pp. 81-84). His main contention is that "current plans of union reflect their origin in a period that is already fading into the past." Hence areas that have changed or are changing must be identified if further discussion and development is to be fruitful.

Dr. Grant contends that the reassertion of the validity of religious pluralism had "significantly dulled the enthusiasm for union"—and lessened concern for a common ground. As I hope my presentation of the theology of the local church makes clear, I find myself in strong agreement here. Added to this is a very large measure of experience drawn from the civil rights structure and minority rights efforts. The whole emphasis here in the United States on ethnic consciousness also may well have something to say on this—the fear that we are endangered by a push toward uniformity that may destroy particular traditions, the fear again of depersonalization and dehumanization, resulting in the outreach to small communities. This kind of consciousness has endangered new and divergent styles of community and religious life. Thus we have a wide spectrum regarding the meaning of religion and of worship. What is important is that any contemporary effort toward ecumenical unity must take pluralism very seriously indeed. If it is taken seriously it seems to me to call for an understanding of the meaning of the ancient medieval title "university." It was "universitas universitatum," a whole of wholes, so that here each ecclesiastical structure is a totality in itself possessing potentialities for a variety of worship and fellowship.

Dr. Grant also points out that in the last two or three years the term "process" has had a dominant role in the discussion of union. Although there are many nuances, it is basically set up in contrast to union. What "process" calls for is joint action now. Implicit or explicit, it would be a critique (hovering on the point of outright rejection) of the stress on a future decision in which union would be jointly voted into existence. First, let me say that the lack of concern for this stress on the future fails to give full meaning to the integral Christian view of the enterprise. Yet it must be recognized "that to a generation single-mindedly caught up in present causes and present experiences" the call for a momentous decision sometime in the future does not spark much enthusiasm. "To such a generation what is not somehow happening now must inevitably appear to be little more than an abstraction" (*art. cit.*, p. 83). As our Columbus experience showed us, "process" is the opening stage that brought the various ecumenical groups together. Yet it seems to me, in the light of that experience and my own reflection, that unless union or communion is seen as an energizing Christian principle, then ecumenical cooperation easily becomes totally secularized and ceases to be an instrument of that unity to which Christ calls us.

(N.B. At this point I had originally planned to discuss Key 73, but I now feel that a full treatment of this would not be directly germane to the purpose of the paper. Moreover, the ways in which the movement is to be implemented are not at all clear and seemed to be clearly determined by the local situation. Its overall ecumenical significance is yet to be judged. However, having raised the issue, it is only fair to say that I personally have real reservations about it. These center in large measure around the description of the movement by some of its proponents as "The Third Great Awakening." This raises for me serious problems concerning what is described in some detail by Martin Marty in his *The Righteous Empire*. Affording even more detail is Robert T. Handy's *A Christian America: Protestant Hopes and Historical Realities*, which is a study of the quest for a Christian America from 1776 to 1920 and what he calls "the second disestablishment" after 1920. I should also like to call attention to some recent critical evaluation of Key 73 in *Christianity and Crisis*, March 19, 1973, where the whole issue was devoted to this topic. Also, most of the Winter 1973 issue of *Dialogue* dealt with Key 73.)

II. *CHURCH AND MINISTRY*

The purpose of this section is not simply to resume again the already existing bilateral studies on ministry. Rather it is to take these studies and their conclusions and set them into the large ecclesiological and ecumenical perspectives being considered in this paper. Perhaps the most effective way to bring this out is the statement of Yves Congar where he points out that during most of his work his basic idea of the fundamental relationship in the Church was priesthood and laity. Now, however, he sees it to be a matter of ministries (services) and community. "We must substitute for the linear schema (Christ—priesthood—faithful) a schema where the community appears as the enveloping reality within which the ministries, even the institutional ministries, are situated as modes of service of what the community is called to be and to do." (Cf. "My Path-Findings in the Theology of Laity and Ministries," *Jurist*, Vol. 32 [Spring 1972], p. 178.)

In the extensive reconsideration of ministry, which has had much of its origin in the ecumenical dialogue, one of the most important factors has been the return to the sources. Thus we have had the confluence of sound historical research and ecumenical actuality. Out of this certain generalizations are possible through which on-going dialogue about the shape of unity may be continued. Certainly, on the Roman Catholic side, there has been the realization that this return to the sources is long overdue. Quite clearly until recent years we have looked at these sources through a kind of entrenched historical conditioning that allowed only certain set observation posts—priests, bishops, Pope. Thus the Pope contained bishops, the bishops contained priests, and priests contained non-priests or laity as a sort of clientele without power. The whole concern in employing the sources was to justify this structure for either internal reasons or what were implicitly polemical or anti-rationalist concerns, and so it became a justification of an established kind of pyramidal form—basically only one priestly ministry but distinct according to jurisdiction. Interior strains, structural stresses, scholarship and ecumenical concern have combined to develop a basic critique of this seemingly monolithic structure. Out of this has come a better understanding of its historical relativities. Because of this critique it is not legitimately possible (in view of the evidence) to identify unconditionally the will or intention of Christ with the juridical and theological constructs of the existing establishment. Certainly Christ formulated elements of doctrine and organization, but its fundamental intentionality was his example: "I am among you as one who serves" (Lk. 22:27).

What has emerged also is the freedom of the apostles to construct structures and forms of function. Clearly it would appear that the only form of ministry formally instituted by Christ was not continued, i.e., the twelve apostles. The New Testament office most emphasized is the apostolate, and that did not endure much beyond the first century. As John McKenzie points out in his article "Ministerial Structures in the New Testament" (*Concilium*, Vol. 74, pp. 13-22), the original pluralism and open-ended situation left by the Twelve allows much scope for ecumenical agreement. Much the same ground is covered by Andre Lemaire in "From Services to Ministries: 'Diakoniai' in the First Two Centuries" (*Concilium*, Vol. 80, pp. 35-49). He gives here some excellent cautionary advice: "The study of the services and ministries of the Church in the first two centuries faces two main difficulties. On the one hand it is always difficult for an historian to grasp a religious movement just as it comes into being, and on the other hand there is a strong temptation to go so far in using the present to reconstruct the past that we project our modern ideas on the early Church" (*ibid.*, p. 35). His article gives extensive reference to a large body of published work in this analysis. To be added is his own most important study, *Les Ministeres au origines de l'Eglise, naissance de la triple hierarchie: eveques, presbyteres, diacres* (Paris 1971). Peter Kearny in the same volume of *Concilium* underlines these conclusions and indicates their ecumenical implications. He would hold that the possibilities for Church order are shaped by "the whole of Church history with special reference to the needs of our day. . . . The potential universality of the Gospel message requires that Church order serve that universality and permit whatever variety of structures best fosters it. . . . The New Testament as a whole is supportive of the view that the various Christian communions, even those without the episcopal order, can be reunited even while retaining their own structures, provided they reach agreement on the basic truths of faith and acknowledge the legitimacy of each other's ecclesial orders." (Cf. "New Testament Incentives for a Different Ecclesial Order?" pp. 62-63; also cf. R. Brown, *Priest and Bishop: Biblical Reflections,* and Hans Küng, *Why Priests?* as well as the review of these two books by Daniel Donovan in his article "Brown, Küng and the Christian Ministry," *The Ecumenist*, Vol. 10, Sept.-Oct. 1972; Y. Congar, "Quelques problemes Touchant les ministeres," *Nouvelle Revue Theologique*, Vol. 93 [1971], pp. 785-800, which also provides an extensive list of writings on this topic.) While from all this it may be argued that questions of office and authority are not central to the Gospel, it would be simplistic not to realize that this is a common ecclesial problem on which all the Christian churches are being interrogated and critically evaluated. To seek out the spirit of the Gospels for a richer understanding of authority and office has become a matter of life and death. What must be brought into full perspective is that Christ is present wherever two or three are gathered in his name. But as J. Colson concludes: "This group must be summoned and meet in the name of Christ, and it is from this that the ministry which summons, assembles and completes the believers in the name of Christ— *in persona Christi*—receives its meaning as a sign. The minister is a sign that the gathering is not merely a human gathering, but a summons by God's grace to believe in his love, the love of which he gave a pledge in the wonderful deeds he performed in Jesus Christ and of which the ministers are no more than the official heralds by preaching and ritual." (Cf. *Concilium*, Vol. 80, "Ecclesial Ministries and the Sacral," p. 74.)

A final point on ministry may be made in keeping with our contemporary climate. While one should not press too heavily on the similarities, still there are common elements between the creative and functional orientations of the New Testament and our own day. It is quite easy to be negative about the decline in vocations, the identity crisis and ministers leaving the ministry. These are facts, but there is another side. The very decline opens the way to new ministries or at least their possibility—the development of new types of vocation, outside the seminary, among adult members of society who come out of a fully formed career. The obvious illustration is the restoration of the diaconate which opens the way to the larger horizon of part-time priests and ministers. Equally important, though facing cultural and emotional problems, is a fully realized and accepted ministry of women. Already in a number of instances women religious are carrying on extensive pastoral activity such as preaching, catechetical formation for adults, and all the functions of a deacon as well as all the functions of a priest except saying Mass, hearing confessions and anointing the sick. Finally there is the increasing scale on which lay people are studying theology academically and the obvious importance of their role now and in the future.

III. *THE CHURCH AND THE WORLD*

The title chosen for this section represents the final ecclesiological perspective to be treated in this paper. The phrase, "The Church and the World" has had a variegated experience in the life of Christianity. The history of this relationship runs from total rejection through ambiguity, through ambivalence, to an extreme acceptance whereby the Church is judged solely on the contribution it can make to the world. At this given moment in our common Christian history, the nature of this relationship sets forth a pervading and objectively inescapable challenge to our common discipleship. This discipleship demands that we bear our witness to the world and fruitfully proclaim to it God's Word. For me, as a professing Christian, we have no choice. This position may not be universally accepted but no effort to shape an ecumenical ecclesiology can ignore the implications of this relation between the Church and the world. Taken in its broadest connotation, the world is not a diverse group of persons over against the believing community. It is the total reality in which man's existence is carried on—believer or not. In this sense Church and world are present simultaneously in each believer's life. This world encompasses, as a dynamic whole, human enterprise interacting with the cosmic order. Thus technical research, scientific and social endeavors, justice and equity are all integral here.

Today, however, this simultaneity of presence involves polarities and tensions that are heatedly debated. The reason for this lies in the history of our Western culture. Humanism, the scientific revolution, the Enlightenment, and the development of national sovereignty have all played their role. What is of primary concern here is what I term for my purposes the *secular* viewed as an *ideology*. As an ideology it rejects both the transcendent and the sacral as purely subjective and unreal. The only relevant notes are physical and historical—and so the contingent and the relative. Everything is on the finite level and there is no place for mystery. The world view that once called for a sacral context is no longer tenable for the convinced secularist. Man is totally dependent on his own resources and powers. Value and meaning are not part of the processes of nature. Man's freedom looks to the future—toward an existence yet to be. The sacral "myths" of the past are unacceptable to science; they bespeak superstition, tend to repress and destroy man's freedom of spirit and action.

At the other end of this spectrum is what Karl Rahner calls "a false integrism" which opposes itself to all legitimate secularization. (Cf. K. Rahner, "Theological Reflections on the Problem of Secularization," *Theology of Renewal*, ed. L. K. Shook, C.S.B., pp. 167-192.) By "integrism" here, Rahner is not referring to the integrism that followed the condemnation of Modernism at the beginning of this century. (Cf. J. O'Brien, "Integralism," *New Catholic Encyclopedia*, Vol. 7, pp. 552-553.) Rather, he has in mind a more or less permanent historical phenomenon that bespeaks a particular attitude and mentality. (For a development of this, cf. A. Michel, "Integrisme," *Dictionnaire Theologie Catholique Tables Generales*, 2294-2304.) What is involved here is a particular attitude and conception of "the Church's relation to the world (in culture, society, and the state) which would reject secularization in all its forms. In this sense integrism is the theoretical or practical attitude according to which the life of man can be projected and directed in every detail from universal principles proclaimed by the Church and controlled by her in their application. An integrism of this kind considers the world and history as the transparent and docile matter in which praxis is nothing but the execution of theory. . . . Integrism supposes that the Church is always in possession of these principles at least sufficiently for all that is of importance; thus it denies that there is a true historical evolution of dogma and theology at least on the level of principles of action. . . . Once it is granted that the Church has the role of proclaiming and interpreting these general principles, so understood, it pertains to her *de jure* (inasmuch as she can lay claim to this right) to direct the world" (*art. cit.*, p. 169).

Between these two extremes of secularism and false integrism we can place a legitimate secularization which Rahner describes as the development of the world and a consequent growing away from the Church. By the Church here he means the historical situation in which religion as an institution and the world formed a relatively homogeneous society. Today, following Vatican II's *Pastoral Constitution in the Church in the Modern World*, Catholics would see this form of secularization as both normal and to be praised. "This Council, therefore, looks with great respect upon all the true, good, and just elements found in the very wide variety of institutions which the human race has established for itself and constantly continues to establish." (Cf. Abbott, *op. cit.*, n. 42 p. 242.)

Finally Pope Paul VI, in his opening address to the Second Session of Vatican II, asserted: "Let the world know this: The Church looks at the world with profound understanding, with sincere admiration and with sincere intention of not dominating it, but of serving it; not of condemning it but of strengthening it and saving it." (Cf. *Council Speeches of Vatican II*, ed. Hans Küng, Y. Congar, D. O'Hanlon, *op. cit.*, p. 234.)

Granted, however, this legitimate understanding of secularization, the need and vocation of the Christian Church to proclaim its witness and God's Word to the secular world demand inescapably that a bridge be built to our contemporary world. I would here suggest for your reflection two areas that seem to me to offer real possibilities. One is the development of new kinds of ecclesial communities that directly react to this issue. The other is the development of Christian theological discourse that will try to confront adequately secularism seen as an ideology.

Ecclesial Communities. The question of community has been raised several times in this paper because of my own conviction that it is an absolutely necessary factor in the dialogue among the Churches and is directly related to the dialogue demanded between the Church and the world. Dr. Kelly in his report on our Columbus study has very effectively presented this point (pp. 17-19). Quoting from R. Nesbit, *The Quest for Community*, he stated: "Man has paid dearly for his breathtaking leap into freedom and now he realizes it: 'Not the free individual but the lost individual, not independence but isolation, not self-discovery but self-obsession—not conqueror but to be conquered.' " Briefly the point at issue here is the growing awareness of the need for a community that looks to the service of our contemporary world. It encompasses a growing awareness that the secularism expressed in Marxism or scientism or humanism, and its demand for collective control of the conditions of life as a viable system of values, is not enough. Despite its claims, the mystery of historical existence and historical evil are not done away with, and the deeper problem of meaning and the questions of ultimacy and transcendence once again are coming to the fore. (Cf. *Time*, April 9, 1973, "Searching Again for the Sacred," pp. 90-93.) One need only recall David Riesman's *The Lonely Nation of Strangers*, presenting these needs in a semi-popular way. What may be inferred out of this whole trend is that Western man (and increasingly the world) is at a point where he seeks to develop a view of himself and his world that takes into account his deeply human drives and needs, and the technological urbanized world that he has developed. In the face of this, many Christians think that the hope for a solution lies with the Church's capacity to create ecclesial communities among the faithful themselves—communities that will be able to live and work with and within the pluralistic society.

The reasons for the kind of thinking seen above are many-sided. Here, however, I should like to indicate a few. Responsible freedom calls for social solidarity, since the development of human personhood and personality—as a stable personal organization for individuals—also calls for some lasting context of beliefs, values and social structure. Is not this the very nature of community? But the whole development of communities, affluence, mobility, and the dynamics of technology make the old system of stability obsolete. (Cf. T. O'Dea, "The Church Returns to Relevance," *Guide*, Vol. VIII (April 1969), pp. 11-16.) Hence, man and, in this thinking, the Church must seek to evolve a community that recognizes this dynamism. This means not simply a toleration of pluralism but learning to live with it and see it as positive and constructive—an amalgam of conservatives and radicals, conformists and non-conformists, people of different political tendencies. To deal with this there must be avoided the strong temptation to integrism. There can be no question of the Church undertaking to transform the secular and pluralist world into a homogeneous society. Such an enterprise would try to make of the Church a ghetto. To avoid this the Church must involve itself in social work in the spirit of collaboration with secular society. Integral to such an approach is the acceptance of the principle of democratization, i.e., that the individual Christian should come to participate in the decision-making processes of the various groupings of the secular society. He must do so because by right he is a member of a whole range of these pluralistic groupings. This is nothing else but the recognition of a far-reaching socio-cultural change. It is no longer simply a question of dealing largely with an illiterate, formless mass, and directing the Church's concern to a small elite and their leadership. Rather the Church must return to an older tradition, the Greek and Roman idea of a *people*, a political notion echoed by St. Thomas. At the base of this notion of people stands "the citizen who feels within himself the consciousness of his own personality, of his duties and rights, and of his due freedom as joined with a respect for the freedom and dignity of others." (Quoted by J. C. Murray, "Religious Freedom," *Concilium*, Vol. 18.)

It is this Christian person who acts in the secular domain and undertakes initiative and involvement as he conscientiously evaluates the actual situation. In the relation of temporal and the spiritual, there is a domain or zone where Christians are called to act as Christians. In this zone the Church does not act by power but by influence. (Cf. G. Martelet, "L'Eglise et le temporal, Vers une nouvelle conception," *L'Eglise de Vatican II* [*Unam Sanctam* 51h]. For a survey of recent literature, cf. Richard A. McCormick, S.J., "The Sociopolitical Mission of the Christian," *Theological Studies*, Vol. 34 [March 1973], pp. 92-102.) The Church's role here is a prophetic one. It will seek to suggest possibilities and solutions without insisting that in the concrete they are the only legitimate solutions. It must recognize that, in the words of Christopher Dawson: "The true social function of the Church . . . is to save civilization from itself by revealing the true end of man and the true end of religion."

The Development of Theological Discourse. Both the legitimacy and the effectiveness of contemporary theological discourse have been under heavy fire for a considerable time. This criticism is not only the kind of total rejection represented by secularism but within the Christian Church itself. Indeed one can quite accurately describe the contemporary problematic of theology as the need to respond to the charge that its language is meaningless even to and in the Church. So Bultmann and his disciples would say that traditional (orthodox) theology is pre-scientific in its understanding of biblical forms. Others, notably Whitehead and Dewart and the whole process theology movement, would see the cause for this obsolescence in the use of Greek and particularly Aristotelian philosophical positions. As they see this, the approach is incapable of handling the contemporary evolutionary understanding of becoming—thus the highly publicized "God is dead" cry made in the name of rationality, freedom, and maturity. Here the whole idea of a search for transcendence in religion is a cause for repression, and in order for man to be free, the "transcendent God" must die.

To all this I should like to indicate a pattern of approach that is very effectively projected in a most stimulating essay by Langdon Gilkey: "Modern Myth-Making and the Possibilities of Twentieth Century Theology," *Theology of Renewal*, Vol. 1 of *Theology of Religious Renewal*. (I have elected to state Gilkey's main thesis and indicate his response to the problem raised rather than develop the whole matter in detail. I do this because of the clarity of his article and to save a lengthy treatment in an area where several professional position papers may well be required.) Gilkey sees his essay as a prolegomenon to theology, and his concern is with myths as his title states. He uses this term not in a perjorative sense of an ancient untrue fable. "Rather it signifies to us a certain mode of language whose elements are multi-valent symbols, whose referent is in some strong way the transcendent or the sacred and whose meanings concern the ultimate or existential issues of actual life and the question of human and historical destiny. Myth is, in other words, to us the appropriate mode of first order religious discourse, and theology is involved in a disciplined reflection upon the mythical language of a historical community or tradition" (p. 283). In the light of this description, Gilkey presents and elaborates a threefold thesis: (1) for the secular ideology, myth and its theological reflection is meaningless intellectually and empirically and so can have no validity; (2) yet, as scholars such as M. Eliade, E. Cassirer, and P. Ricoeur have shown, myths and symbolic language are vital to a culture, and secularism itself has myths and slogans that are not explicitly admitted intellectually but are present existentially for self-understanding; (3) finally, Christian theology, reflecting on the myths and symbols of the Christian community, "provides the best basis for the self-understanding of secular culture." and so can give to it "a sense of identity and relevance and integrity in relation to its historical, traditional function," and so give meaningfulness for a new secular age (*ibid.* pp. 283-284). As Gilkey sees it, secular existence raises ultimate questions to which only myth and symbolic language can respond—those secular myths that are in fact evolved and eviscerated by the incapacity of the secular mind to think symbolically and so cannot comprehend the enigmas of life. Such things as mystery, the transcendent and the sacred escape it because the secular mind cannot encompass fruitfully the meaningfulness and creative character of destiny. (Cf. *ibid.*, pp. 308-309.)

Symbolism. Implied in all this matter is the profound reality of symbol—the correlative aspect of mythical thinking. The reason for introducing it here is that it touches on a deep but often not too conscious ecumenical concern—the liturgy. "Myth . . . has the purpose of providing grounds for the ritual actions and thought by which a man understands himself and his world. . . . But in losing its explanatory pretense the myth reveals its explanatory *significance* (italics mine) and its contribution to understanding . . . its symbolic function . . . its power of discovering and revealing the bond between man and what he considers sacred." (Cf. P. Ricoeur, *The Symbolism of Evil*, p. 5.) Applying this to the liturgy, one can understand how much of a role it can play in bearing witness to Christians living in a secularized world. By its nature the liturgy is called to be an all-embracing sign of the basic relation that we, as believers, have with God revealing himself through Christ and celebrating his paschal mystery. Yet there is a solid corpus of contemporary experience that is not at all satisfied with the present state of Christian liturgy. Some want it to be almost totally archeologistic. Others feel that liturgical symbolism is so subjective that it is purely transient. Still others have neither a conscious concern nor an interest in the whole liturgical experience. Yet if worship is the proper center of our understanding and relation to the sacred, is there not a necessary demand for ecumenical study and reflection on it? It is not here a question of establishing a uniform liturgical expression. Room for different traditions and ritual emphasis must be allowed. What is needed is both academic study and educational renewal that would represent a common ecumenical enterprise. For here we must reach into the very roots of religious experience and its meaning. It means making our own the extensive resources that religious anthropology has opened for us. (Cf. especially Mircea Eliade, *Patterns in Comparative Religion; Cosmos and History; The Sacred and the Profane, Images and Symbols;* "Methodological Remarks on the Study of Religious Symbolism," *The History of Religions*, ed. by Mircea Eliade and Joseph Kitawagwa; also Louis Dupre, *The Other Dimension: A Search for the Meaning of Religious Attitudes*, which is a personal synthesis of the basic themes of the religious phenomenon and its root in human experience; also of special value here are the articles of William Van Roo, S.J., "Symbol According to Cassirer and Langer," *Gregorianum*, Vol. 53 [1972], pp. 334-487 and 615-677. These are valuable because Van Roo is seeking to establish the context of a theory of symbol to study the functions of Christian sacrament as symbol in a work now being prepared.)

The permanent value of this whole approach is incalculable to one for whom religion is a true and deep concern. Religious experience to be communicated is ineluctably dependent on symbolic expression. In a peculiarly intensive way the contemporary religious mind is faced with the necessity of refashioning and relating traditional symbols to new conditions. The intensity of this problem derives from the fact that the mentalities to whom the older symbols were addressed differ so strikingly from the minds that are trained in today's world.

Specifying and giving direction to this need for understanding symbolism and its relation to the sacred is the contemporary existential emphasis on sign as a participatory expression of man's very nature as man. This position is both a reaction to and a rejection of the idealist dichotomy between man and his world. In contrast to this is the affirmation that if man is to grow and develop, his own reality as man must be directed to and interrelated with his world. To become fully human, man must relate meaningfully to the world of persons and things in which he lives. There can be no authentic human growth save that being a man means becoming a man. Becoming a man is "a process in which a man gives himself to the world and grows up in that process." If this is to occur, a man must realize that of necessity he is in a symbolic situation. To be a person man must express his personal interior reality to the world. To do this means his interior reality is expressed in bodily signs and gestures whereby the world of matter participates in his personal development. Man knows himself only insofar as he has made himself to be by reason of his world and his historicity in it. The world is a necessary means for his personal growth. It is, therefore, by his sign-acts that he expresses himself to the world and so grows in his own personhood. His very human bodiliness is the sign of his personal reality. Seen this way, a sign is not an accidental cloak for an idea but its necessary and essential organ. The sign expresses man's personal interior to the world and its bodiliness is the very self-expression of the spirit. (Cf. K. Rahner, "Toward a Theology of Symbols," *Theological Investigations*, Vol. IV, pp. 255ff.)

To a scholastically trained mind (like my own) what has just been presented almost automatically inspires a wariness that there is here a dangerous potential for complete subjectivism. I think this is a legitimate worry, but I am also aware that at base it is not only a philosophical issue but one of the problems of being a human being. Despite this danger the contemporary existential approach can play a very fruitful role in considering the problems raised and (liturgically) to be raised. What sets it in the forefront is the mystery of the human person. Man is not simply an object in his world that is a given. Rather by reason of the historicity of his existence and the employment of his personal freedom in building the world, man can be a truly decisive factor. Here is represented one of the *givens* of secularization in its concern for the creative character of human freedom. Through this it challenges the world rather than being engulfed by it. (Cf. M. R. Barral, *Merleau-Ponty, The Role of the Body-Subject in Interpersonal Relations*; also K. Rahner, *ibid.*, pp. 255ff. and L. Gilkey, *art. cit.*, pp. 289-290.)

What I have covered very schematically is what in the phenomenological and existential perspective constitutes the structure in which "meaning" is conceived. It is not simply a kind of abstract value that we assign to a particular complex of elements. Rather it is the basic mutual relationship between man and the world in which he exists. What value the world has for a man, and what he sees has value to it, is what meaning is. He does not create these values, but it is equally important to recognize that the world has no discernible meaning apart from the human mind. Existentially, in this sense, man's life is a continuous symbolization.

This material about myth and symbol and sign is intended here only to suggest something of a contemporary context for reflection on liturgical worship. I say here "suggest" since at this present point its only purpose is to propose a possible approach in an area that presses upon Christians in any discussion of the Church and the world. Watching television commercials, and all too many of its programs, we see how many symbols have become impoverished if not debased. The same is true in liturgical action, where the realities that word and sacrament seek to signify can be corroded by a usage that leaves untouched both their sacred and their human and personal depths. It is always too easy to think that change in actions or forms will by that fact make the permanent symbols expressing revelation real. To one who as a Roman Catholic priest has been strongly sympathetic with the liturgical renewal inaugurated officially at Vatican II, this kind of occupational hazard has been again and again recognizable in a situation offering a wide range of innovative possibilities—the seminary liturgies. All too often the whole emphasis has been on the horizontal—the human, the familial, the personal, it has left almost imperceptible the vertical—the sacred, the transcendent, the very centrality of Christian worship. With this in mind I suggest some possible considerations for further discussion. (Cf. The Fourth Assembly of World Council of Churches at Uppsala [1968] which considered a draft document on the worship of God in a secular age [Geneva 1968]. In view of this, Faith and Order held a consultation [September 1969] on worship in a secularized world. The recommendations of the consultation were published in *Studia Liturgica* 7 [1970], Nos. 2-3.)

Faith and the Liturgy. Here, consonant with the purpose of this paper, I am concerned directly with Christian worship and its Christian tradition. The first step that leads to the birth of liturgical worship is the kerygma. Here, regarding the New Testament, kerygma is the proclamation of the Good News—it is the proclamation of the saving event but as interpreted for the hearer. It is at once sacred event and its saving meaning, but the kerygma not only projects to the whole man who hears but seeks to encompass the preacher also who seeks to express and participate in a common faith. Effective through the Spirit, the kerygma seeks to lead a man to respond to the event in faith—personal and existential. He moves in love and hope and trust and the beginnings of commitment. Yet (in the context of what we have seen concerning sign) this inner personal experience of a man only becomes authentically human when it is given expression—form. It is through this sign-act that he participates fully in the event to which he responds. Thus the words and the symbols of the liturgy are the more important expressions of faith because they concern the whole man. "Liturgical expression is therefore an essential aspect of faith causing it to become an act." (Cf. G. Lukken, "The Unique Expression of Faith in the Liturgy," *Concilium*, Vol. 82, pp. 11-21; also A. Greeley, "Religious Symbolism, Liturgy and Community," *Concilium*, Vol. 62, pp. 59-69.) It may be helpful in illuminating all this by introducing the early Eastern Church's description of the liturgy as *theologia prima* and speculative theology as *theologia secunda*. By this is meant that liturgy in which faith gives expression to itself is the first source and norm, for it is here that God gives himself to man and man gives himself through Christ. It is so much richer than the *theologia secunda*, yet constant dialogue is called for. (Cf. G. Lukken, *art. cit.*, pp. 19-20.) A similar notion is found fairly early in the fifth-century Western Church in the axiom, "Lex supplicandi lux orandi." (Cf. Denzinger-Schonmetzer, *Enchiridion Symbolorum*, Nos. 246, 3792, 3828.)

The Holy. The reason for taking up here the idea of "the Holy" is that in religion it is the objective element of what we have been seeing in terms of faith and liturgy. Sign and symbol seek to witness to and bespeak the reality of our encounter with the Holy freely giving itself. The Holy, as used here, is the central concept of comparative religion and thus of the history of man's religious experience. Moreover the uniqueness of the Holy has been a part not only of man's religious experience but of his conscious conviction. The works of E. Durkheim and R. Otto, and of Max Scheler and his philosophy of values, have made this very much a necessary and central concern of any discussion of religion. For "concern with the Holy rather means seeking the domain or dimensions proper to the divine encounter in which the supreme principle shows itself." (Cf. K. Hemmerle, "Holy," *Sacramentum Mundi*, Vol. 3, p. 51.) Crucial to understanding "the Holy" is the fact that it is not to be conceived in terms of an abstract attribute. Rather, it is, as Hemmerle writes, a question of "encounter" (*ibid.*). To the Christian this encounter is the historical moment where the Holy, the Divine Principle, manifests itself in the unique revelation in Jesus. I say here "to the Christian" because by nature the Holy is not something co-extensive only with Christianity. It is interwoven with man's awareness of being as well as himself and thus is expressed in a variety of human ways and forms. This very multiplicity is itself important to the Christian thinker because the revelation in which he believes presupposes on the part of man ontic openness to God's self-giving. The horizon of the Holy is addressed by revelation. (It is this that M. Blondel articulated so strikingly in his *L'Action*. One finds it in the whole school of transcendental Thomism. Of particular importance here would be Karl Rahner's *Hearers of the Word*.)

What this means in terms of the whole problematic underlying this final section of this paper is summed up forcefully by L. Gilkey: "[In what we call] the contemporary crisis of faith [there are manifested] most fundamentally of all the elusiveness for all of us in our time of the Holy, the absence of countless persons with a vivid sense of the presence of the Divine —an absence felt not only in our daily life in the world but (even more devastating) an absence brought from the world into our holy places and experiences when Christians gather together in worship. This absence of deity in our common worship contributes to and even founds our other religious and theological problems . . . for affirmation in faith of the reality of God and discourse about him alike depend upon an experience of his living presence. Thus the reality of common worship is the center on which depend both Christian religious existence and Christian theology." (Cf. L. Gilkey, "Addressing God in Faith," *Concilium*, Vol. 82, pp. 62-63.) In response to this powerful critique, I would see a call for a return to the very rich and beautiful Christian tradition of the *sacrament*. By that I mean what is the common religious experience of man given a powerful and unique significance for us in and by the incarnation. Here the presence of God, the Holy, is seen in the fully human personality of Jesus. To the Christian it speaks in a unique mode about what religious experience has been so aware of—that God's presence is in and through his activity in the world (be it nature or history or events or men). Here is what Edward Schillebeeckx means when he uses the words "Christ the sacrament of our encounter with God." Thus in the Christian tradition and its historical community the person of Jesus is the significant and supreme symbol of the presence of God—the Holy. So also the Christian Church may by analogy be called a sacrament. For the invisible principle that animates the Church is that same Spirit which also animates the humanity of Christ. "The Church thus becomes the sacrament of salvation in imitation of Christ the head. It develops a special ('pneumatic') structure of its own in all the forms which are proper to it as a social structure in the Spirit. This view of the Church is just as important as the basic fact that it is founded and constituted from on high by grace." (Cf. A. Grillmeier, *art. cit.*, p. 149.)

Here then, within the Christian community, divine presence, kerygma, Word and sacrament are called to interact and find their point of interaction in our common Christian worship. Thus baptism and the Eucharist re-present for us the events in which the community originates. Word and kerygma seek to make effective these symbols by invoking their transcendent meaning so that they may communicate the Holy to us. In their most powerful moments different emphases of the Protestant and Catholic traditions have always done this. Word and sacrament sometimes overemphasize. While having only minimal experience of Protestant worship, it is not possible for me, having heard ministers proclaiming the Word or having read a good deal of the preaching tradition of the Reformation, to remain unaware of the power of the Word to open the Holy to men. As a Catholic I cannot help but feel that for my generation, and those before me and so many after me, no more powerful experience of the Holy can be found than in the elevation of the host and the chalice at Mass. It is equally clear to me now that while the traditions have been diverse they are not mutually exclusive. In fact our shared experience of these last few years forces us to realize that, theologically, a fully activated worship that brings into vital interrelation the Holy, the personal, and the community must affirm that Word and sacrament not only complement one another but are incomplete without each other. To ignore or to underplay the sacramental element and to replace it with only reflection and moral concepts is to render almost null any possibility of a celebration of the Holy and of the transcendent. In short it fails to present the deepest meaning of why we worship. Equally, if the Word is not fully present calling for reflection, understanding, decision and commitment, then the sacramental reality can become merely a matter of form or unhappily border on the magical. "The clue to renewed worship as of a renewed Christian existence and theology, insofar as by reflection we can take care of these matters, is to reappropriate through the forms of Christian symbolism the presence of the holy in the totality of ordinary existence." (Cf. L. Gilkey, *art. cit.*, p. 70.)

In the course of writing this paper I have become more and more convinced that in attempting to conceive of the shape of the unity we seek we are being given a charismatic challenge and a charismatic opportunity. The signs of the times appear to indicate that the Christian Church is becoming an increasingly minority factor and may well be on its way to becoming a *diaspora*. The temptation is and will be to turn inward and protect what we have like a kind of new Ark. Yet a truly ecumenical view of the Church and its mission precludes this. My own feeling was expressed a half century ago by Max Scheler in his work *On the Eternal in Man* written shortly after World War I: "Consider the person who merely wishes to preserve or at the most defend his religious position: if he dare not see in it the positive means of salvation for suffering humanity and will not extend to humanity this means in a gift of joy and love, then he will find that even his more modest goal of self-preservation is no longer attainable. As men reckon, his cause will vanish from the face of the earth."

Eugene M. Burke

Community and Institutional Factors in the Shape of the Unity We Seek

SOCIOLOGICAL INPUT—BI-LATERAL CONSULTATION
COLUMBUS, OHIO

1.0 *INTRODUCTION TO OUR SITUATION*

1.1 *The Method of This Project*

Bi-lateral conversations between Roman Catholics and other Protestant denominational families have had their origins in the methods of Faith and Order dialogue. This method tends to be deductive and based upon historical and scriptural antecedents. As such, the conversations have tended to revolve around the points of theology and ecclesiology which have divided us. This particular bi-lateral has had a broader base than some, however, with antecedent conversations both on theological issues, and in worship and mission.

At the last meeting of the Reformed Family and Roman Catholic Bilateral, it was decided that the conversations for the ensuing three years should focus around the nature of the unity we seek. This is a projective task. It must be based upon historical antecedents, but could also be based on contemporary experience. Therefore, the consultation decided to focus its energies on the ecumenical styles and experiences of a target metropolitan area. The purpose was to discover what the contemporary ecumenical experience is that has drawn us together. The method of approach for this endeavor was through participant observation and group interviews. The purpose of this process was to discover from grass-roots ecumenical experience clues about the real issues of ecumenical life and work, and to use this as the basis of discussion of the future shape of unity.

In January 1973, a study team of four persons, including a sociologist, a theologian, an ecumenist and a lay person went to Columbus, Ohio for six days. During that time, they interviewed and/or participated with persons from seventeen different ecumenical expressions. The interviews were semi-structured, with lead questions in four areas of concern: (1) What were the forces which gave rise to the ecumenical activity? (2) What are the blockages and problems which the group faced? (3) What were the theological/ecclesiological foundations which gave rise to the group, and how have your theological perceptions about the Church been modified by the experience? (4) What do your experiences have to say about the future shape of the Church?

From these interviews each member of the team put together their reflections. Then the team came together for interaction and reflection to discover the generalized learnings. These learnings are reflected in the theological and sociological papers presented to the bi-lateral.

1.2 *The Theological Perspective From Which the Sociological Paper Is Written*

Sociology is a study of the associations, institutions, social systems and cultures which have developed from human interaction. The sociology of religion focuses in particular upon the religious institution, values and roles. Like most social sciences, sociology or sociology of religion is not value-free. Those who practice the "art" of sociology have value assumptions. The general framework of this writer's value assumptions follows:

1.2.1 *The Fundamental Theological Assumptions*

1. That God is the Creative Being and his purposes are creative and redemptive.
2. That the objective manifestation of God's creative activity is creation— the universe and all the things in that universe, including mankind. (Change is inherent in the concept of creation as "process," i.e., creation is incomplete and is yearning for completion.)
3. That creation is an on-going process.
4. That the nature of creation requires wholeness—the opposite, anti-creation, can be theologically categorized as sin.

5. That humankind is endowed with freedom which allows it the choice to participate in anti-creation processes.

1.2.2 *The Creator and Creation in Interaction*

God is essentially the initiator and sustainer of the on-going creation. Creation is the objective manifestation of God's creative activity. *Creation* means all that exists in the dimension of time and space. It is that which God has created and as such is variously called "history," "society," "milieu," or "time and space."

God's nature is purposeful. He has provided creation not only with freedom, but also with the possibility of redemption or fulfillment.

Even though the natural order of creation reflects something of the Creator's plan, there are forces at work which run counter to the dominant trends of the Creator's will and intentions. The opposite of creation, with its yearning for wholeness and order, is chaos or anti-creation. Of all the created order, humankind is most demonstrably free to choose to become a participant in creation with the Creator, or to be a participant in the anti-creation process. The latter category is given the theological name of "sin," while the former is called "redemption," i.e., the purposeful direction of man's will toward the dominant trends.

1.2.3 *Humankind, the Highest Order of Creation*

Five things can be affirmed regarding humankind as a factor in the state of creation. First, it is the nature of man to be an individual. Second, it is inherent in man's nature to be a part of a community and a society, and for him to order his life in predictable patterns. Third, there is something deep in man that makes him respond to wholeness, order, beauty, and creation. The religious institution yearns to collaborate with God, the nature of man is to be free to discern and recognize God through the activity of the Holy Spirit in creation. Man's disobedience and the incomplete redemption of creation frequently cause man to limit his own opportunity because of the entangling social structures he weaves in his attempts to give order to his existence. These social structures often leave him insensitive to the creation process. This is social sin or corporate anti-creation. The fifth affirmation is that man is ultimately free and responsible and able to decide whether or not to love God.

1.2.4 *The Church as Product of Social-Theological Interaction*

The premises intertwined in the section above give rise to some foundation premises regarding the order of society and the relationship of the

Church to that ordered pattern. The basic foundation statements are:

1. That the order developed by humankind through the dimensions of time has produced civilizations.
2. That civilizations are systems of social structures devised so that man can function in a whole and orderly way in creation.
3. That social structures (institutions) can function to "free" man for interaction with and participation in creation. Social structures (institutions), on the other hand, can also be divisive and be instrumental in man's participation in anti-creation.
4. That the Church is a people whose purpose and will is to participate in the creation process. Religious social systems or institutions are the vehicles by which these people are nurtured in their allegiance toward active participation in creation.
5. That religious institutions are the means by which these people demonstrate the feasibility of participation in the on-going creation process at all levels of a civilization. Therefore, the purpose of the religious institution we call the Church, both as a people and as an institution, is to move the social systems, and ultimately the civilization, toward participation in creation as opposed to anti-creation.

Summary—In summary, I submit that:

a. The Church is not a polity, a tradition, an institutional form, or an ethos.
b. The Church is a free people who by choice live under a divine imperative. The Church is the result of a qualitative (redemptive) relationship among its central actors. These include: God, the Creator, through Jesus Christ, Man, and the stage of man's being which is variously called creation, history or environment.
c. The nature of society is such that it demands a form by which "dynamic ideas" may be communicated to man's need. Therefore, the institution that we know as the Church provides the structure whereby men living under the divine redemptive imperative may have fellowship with each other. It also provides the structure, or vehicle, through which man may focus his resources so that they will have an impact upon the whole marketplace of man.
d. Denominationalism is essentially the result of faithfully focusing the resources of the people of God to meet the needs of a given socio-historical situation.
e. Although man's basic needs are universal and timeless, the expression of these needs are in constant, but frequently predictable flux. The categories which express man's basic needs and entanglements change and cause the status quo institutional structure to become obsolete.
f. Therefore, the Church to be faithful to its imperatives has no other

choice than to continually "trade in" its obsolete vehicle on vehicles which can successfully focus its resources to make an impact on the marketplace.

Summary Proposition: The essential nature of the Church is that it is one in locality regardless of the social or historical differentiation factors which might separate it. Its uniqueness lies in the fact that it purports to be the redemptive agency in society. Its unity arises from the factors which it holds in common. These include the message and man's basic estrangement from himself, his God, and his fellow men.

1.3 *The Cultural Situation*

This perspective gives rise to the next concern.

It is: What are the characteristics of the historical and societal context in which contemporary redeemed man is being called to be the Church? The corollary question is: What does our understanding of what it means to be Christian in the context of the contemporary world indicate about the shape of the unity we seek?

1.3.1 *Pluralism*

We have emerged from the 1960's aware of the real pluralism, diversity and conflict inherent in our society. The veneer has been peeled off our American way of life. The fundamental diversity of self-interests which underlies that veneer has been exposed. Some of the basic operating myths on which our society has been built have been called into question. The representative principle, whereby one person represents 400,000+ diverse persons, who by historical accident occupy the same geographic turf, is not working well. Minority self-interest groups have developed a sense of identity, and are no longer satisfied to allow others to make their decisions for them. We have undergone some basic reformulation of how we function as a society, both in relationship to each other internally, and in relationship to the rest of the world.

At the same time there is a real mood in a counter direction—a mood toward consolidation, a mood to conserve. These two trends are creating a new scene which affects not only our society, but also the churches. New major coalitions of power and influence are emerging.

Time was when WASP described the broad influential middle class. Other white ethnic groups, many of whom were Orthodox, Roman Catholic, or even Jewish, were excluded. The former tended to be Republican and the latter were coalesced in the Democratic Party. Today many of the latter groups are finding that their needs and values are being threatened just like those of the former WASPs. There now seems to be emerging a new coalition of former ethnics and WASPs into a powerful and influential middle America which has not yet been captured by either political party.

In ecumenical circles we are increasingly seeing these groups coalesce. It is not uncommon to find ecumenical action organizations with Roman Catholics, mainline Protestants, Jewish and Orthodox constituents. Increasingly, we are finding it difficult to find meaningful liaison with black denominations and other minority ethnic groups, such as the Chicano and American Indian. With the black denominations the problem is not so much with the traditional titular heads, but with their constituency. They see us—and rightly so—as the oppressor, as the man, as the enemy. The new coalition holds the power which, through corporate sin, oppresses. It is the American dilemma, in a new form, which we have been unable or unwilling to transcend.

Forces are pulling us both ways. The ultimate configuration this will take in the Church is not yet known. We can, however, take note of these forces and speculate on their implications for the future of both the denomination and the ecumenical future. In the language of group process, we can "force field" the trends, and perhaps "see through a glass darkly," i.e., catch a glimpse of the future.

1.3.1.1. *Forces of Convergence in Our Pluralism*

A. The prophetic response of the 1960's caused the demise of the 1970's. There is now a common need to "pull" together by capturing anew our common heritage and calling as Christians. We have the potential of welding a new coalition between personal faith and corporate witness.

B. The common question of ultimate survival. This includes both ecological survival and the survival of a new way of life in relation to the badly torn social fabric.

C. The emerging middle-class values are increasingly superseding the ethnic values which divided us in the past. The new pluralistic milieu is allowing us to define our common ground in a new way—to draw a larger circle.

D. The need for institutional survival. The bureaucracies of the various denominations have sensed institutional stress and disorganization. Their professional and corporate self-interest is threatened. This is giving new motivation for a more institutionally responsive mode of action. To survive will require consolidation of resources. In some cases this will be done across denominational boundaries—although probably not via denominational mergers. For example, the United Church of Christ and the United Methodist Church have merged their social action magazines into one called "Engage/Social Action."

E. Because of the pragmatic experiences of discipleship we are realizing the folly of historical theological arguments which are shadows of the conflicts of another time.

F. In the 1960's we affirmed that our vocation was to deal with the corporate world. This has now pulled us apart to the extent that you couldn't distinguish the Christian vocation from that of any other agent of social change. Therefore, in the 1970's there is a convergence around theology, the person, salvation, and the renewal of the Church. We are saying that only as we have identity as Christians, and as groups of Christians, can we have authenticity as persons and as corporate actors.

G. A final positive force—although it could be argued to the contrary—is the emergence of a new localism. At best this is bearing responsibility where it should be borne. It is helping us distinguish what functions really belong at which level of society; it is forcing a new accountability. At the same time there are forces of proliferation which will affect the denominations, their judicatory styles and functions, and ultimately their ecumenical work.

1.3.1.2 *Proliferating Forces in Our Pluralism*

A. The Torn Social Fabric: The late 1960's liberated many social forces which are counter to the mainstream style of Americanism, as well as to well-ordered Church life. Although there are signs that these are increasingly being integrated into the systems of our society, the stress and discomfort they cause will be with us for some time—as well they should. Some forces have been driven underground and will certainly be heard from again. The real tragedy lies in the fact that many of these counter-movements represent the creativity our society so desperately needs. Without their active antagonism our whole society could stultify, and in Toynbeeian terms may make us "ripe" for radical revolution.

B. The current efforts at consolidation in society and in the Church could become the means of perpetuating the status quo. In an era of rapid communication and rapid transportation, the status quo, in either Church or society, is tantamount either to ultimate discontinuity, anti-creation (sin) and unproductive conflict, or to a withering, arrested society because of the unmet challenges of pluralism.

C. The exclusive personal spiritual renewal, such as the charismatic movement, the pentecostal movement, the Jesus movement, and Eastern
religious styles of meditation cut across all organized religion. But if
research on the current mood of these is indicative, these may be
fraught with many counter-productive dangers. Although they cut
across the religious community in a new way, perhaps expanding it,
the alternative danger lies in what these movements may become. Current research tends to point to: (1) apocalypticism, (2) salvationism, in
the escape sense, (3) the following of a single charismatic leader with
little democratic recourse, (4) a strict pietistic discipline, and (5) a new
language which makes communication with the total culture very difficult.

D. Pluralism itself can be a proliferating force, unless we learn that only
out of diversity can come real unity. The danger lies in the tendency in
our society to force our pluralistic diversity into a uniformity which
will produce further covert, if not overt, conflict and ultimately more
serious dysfunction in our culture.

E. Finally there is a crisis of values in our society. Values give meaning to
life. Commonly held values make it possible for us to meet real day-
to-day problems creatively. The current tragedy lies in the fact that
our societal values are obsolete. They have to do with personal worth,
hard work, efficiency, profit, consumption, manifest destiny, etc. The
historical context has changed and in our pluralism we have not been
able to develop values to deal with our contemporary situation. This
means that with no workable values we have a state of "anomie" or
normlessness. In this state of affairs there is no means to judge behavior. Without the cement of common values the centrifical force of pluralism will cause proliferation to intensify.

1.3.2 *The Historical Context*

Some fascinating observations have been made by historians regarding the rise and fall of societies, cultures and nations. Some societies have
remained dynamic almost indefinitely; others have been arrested and continue in a crystallized state; still others have died and disappeared. Western Christian civilization is now confronting the hard blows wrought externally by the Third World, which controls much of the world's not yet
developed human and natural resources, while internally it is confronting
its own problems with a super-heated consumptive economic style. Its institutions are having difficulty coping with the human problems which

have emerged in the complex technological society. There sometimes seems to be a feeling of panic that no one is in control. A kind of frenzied fibrillation is evident.

The issue which our civilization confronts is: Will we respond to the creative minority of our society and make the social investment to incorporate this creativity, in an evolutionary fashion, into the dominant culture, or, in our frustration, will we oppress· the creative potential, affirm the status quo, and let our society either die or be overrun and destroyed from the outside? In Toynbeeian terms, if we move toward the latter, we, like societies before us, may leave for our successor society only a unified religion. This context has significant implications for the function, role and shape of the unity we seek as Christians.

It is in this kind of milieu that we are called upon to define the shape of the unity we seek. The task is now one of looking in more depth at its implications in terms of the themes which emerged in the Columbus, Ohio interviews. Essentially the sociological themes which were delineated there for further exploration included: institutionalism, the contemporary context of community and the role of leadership in the Church.

2.0 *The Instiition*

An institution is the result of a creative idea about how you can meet a basic human need which has taken on a structural form. An institution belongs to its constituency. Its being is rooted in the needs of its constituency. Therefore, the institution exists to make it possible, through a symbiotic process, for people to meet their needs. Further, it provides the means by which its resources can be focused, to share with others the creative idea (myth). This is to say that the institution becomes the carrier of certain perceptions of reality and values which it communicates to succeeding generations of its own constituency and to the larger community. Thus, the institution is always the means, it is not the end. When the means becomes the end, the institution is dysfunctional.

The Columbus interviews have brought particular insight into the institutional factors of the unity we seek. Generally, we learned that you can't erase history, all institutions are not at the same point in their development and when an institution is no longer functionally meeting its constituency's needs, and is unwilling to change, it will be by-passed. Specifically, there were insights into the functions, the life cycle, and the role of underlying myths of the religious instiition that came from the Columbus experience and that need to be explored in the shape of the unity we seek.

2.1 *The Function of the Religious Institution*

The religious system in Columbus provides a variety of internal and external functions for its constituency and for the community. The internal functions could generally be described as the nurture function and the outreach function. Nurture includes all that is done to enhance the relationships of the community of faith with each other and with the Creator. The outreach function is the provision which the religious institution makes for the persons of faith to focus their resources so that they can "impact" the larger community. These two functions are in tension with each other. If one is engaged in to the exclusion of the other, an imbalance occurs which is not helpful.

The external functions have to do with the expectations of the larger community for the religious systems. The larger community expects the religious institution to function as its conscience. This is the prophetic role. At the same time the larger community expects the religious institutional system to help it conserve those values which it has found to be useful to its continued maintenance. This is the conserving function. Likewise, these two external functions must be kept in tension with each other. To engage in the conserving function to the exclusion of the conscience function is to reify the culture. The product would be a cultural religion or a folk religion. To engage only in the prophetic function to the exclusion of the conserving function would be to cut off credibility in the larger community.

In Columbus, we discovered that not all religious institutions were engaged equally in each of these functions. Yet, when all of the institutions in the metropolitan religious system were seen as a totality, they tended to function in a complementary manner so that the system was relatively well balanced. This is to say that some were engaged in nurture, others in outreach, while still others were conserving and still others were prophetic. Thus, even within the religious system there was a complementary or symbiotic relationship.

2.2 *The Institutional Life Cycle*

A second observation which arises out of the Columbus research is that the religious institution in general and the ecumenical expression in particular has a life cycle. Essentially the cycle appears to have the following periods:
1. Need in the community leads a concerned few to organize (form a formal association).

2. The period of slow growth—the community is standing back to see if it is going to succeed in meeting real needs.

3. Demonstration of real "life"—"conquest growth." The community has accepted the institution because it has shown that it can meet the community's needs.

4. Membership plateau—the institution sustains an average that reflects the fluctuations in the community. It is meeting the needs of the persons in the community that it has traditionally served.

5. The decisive third—the institution fails to adapt to the changing community needs; thus it tends not to attract the new people who are taking the place of those who die. Minor adjustments needed.

6. The crucial third—if minor adjustments are not made above, the institution will further get out of touch with reality. Here radical redefinition of purpose, and new leadership must emerge or frustration and resulting apathy will continue the downward trend.

7. The fatal third—if adaptations were not made the result will be a small crystallized socio-religious grouping of "our kind of people" totally unconcerned about "mission" or meeting needs. Introverted and self-satisfied. Concerned only to keep the institutional doors open.

8. Dissolution—the most creative possibility is dissolution.

For example, Church Women United had reached a point of relative crystallization and dysfunctional organizational style. They are now in the process of redirecting their life into more appropriate directions. If they don't they will crystallize into a small self-serving group. The Ohio Council of Churches and the Metropolitan Area Church Board, on the other hand, have just come through this kind of radical redirection. They have created new myths about how you engage in ministry ecumenically. This has caught the imagination of the constituency because it brought new creativity into a previously dysfunctional style. At this writing it would appear that both have "struck their stride" and are functioning in a pattern similar to that described in State 4 above.

Still, some of the ecumenical organizations are just now beginning to create their reason for being—their motivating myth—and are now trying to prove their worth and value to constituency (Stages 2 and 3 above). In Columbus, these were represented by the Catholic charismatics, the black ministers' group, some of the neighborhood clusters and the seminary cluster. There is some indication that some of the latter groups have not succeeded, and will have their growth arrested, while others seem to be catching the imagination of the constituents.

Thus, the life cycle becomes both a description and an analytical device. It shows that the participant expectations, functionality and operational issues and problems are not the same for each organization. Where an organization is in its life cycle it will predict how it will respond to a variety of possible crisis. This is true in part because value styles are also inherent in the cycle.

2.3 *Myth, Values and Ideology*

Not only does an institution go through an institutional cycle, but it also goes through a cycle in relationship to the value forces which carry it. In the early stages of its life an organization develops its common perception of reality (myth) which, in turn, can meet the needs of the core constituency, and is the basis by which they generate, in common, their fantasy, dreams, goals and actions that make them viable. These myths and their resulting interaction with the larger community are based upon values. With continued common experience, these myths and values begin to have a patterned interacting response within and between constituency and the larger community. This patterning becomes normative at about Stage 4. From Stage 4 on, the patterned values and myths are highly rational and become institutionalized into formal ideology or dogma. However, the roots of this patterned ideology are in the earlier historical setting which gave rise to the organization. Yet history is continually changing the setting. Thus, although old patterns are normative, as you move further through the cycle they are increasingly dysfunctional to the contemporary situation. This causes deviation—breaking with the normative—and without modification of the normative ideology to better fit contemporary needs, people of creative vitality will leave the institution, and it will become a "holding action" of a few self-serving individuals.

As indicated above, the Catholic charismatics, the seminary cluster, and several of the neighborhood clusters are just now beginning to develop the common values, aspirations and goals which catch the imagination of a constituency. The Ohio Council of Churches and the Metropolitan Area Church board, both of which have emerged with creative new thrusts from relatively crystallized institutional forebears, have their motivating myths defined. Both are currently patterning their expectations, myths, beliefs and goals into norms of expectation and behavior.

Church Women United has a well-developed normative pattern with its resultant ideologies (which they realize must be modified). For the most part it would appear that ecumenical agencies are not frequently afforded the luxury of crystallized self-serving and its supporting dogma because they tend to be at least two steps away from the pocketbook—i.e., ecumenical agencies tend to belong to other institutions (local churches, judicatories, etc.). (Perhaps an exception which does exist in Columbus is the Protestants and Other Americans United for Separation of Church and State, although the bi-lateral team did not interview them.) The general observation about the function of values, myths, beliefs, ideology and dogma is that they play a dynamic role in the shaping of institutions.

2.4 Cultural and Institutional Impediments

2.4.1 Internal Impediments

The experience in Columbus dramatizes the fact that ecclesiastical organization is a means and not an end. Where it provides a means to respond to the real felt needs of the people, it is utilized. The data in Columbus strongly indicate, however, that where the institution becomes a block and impedes participation in meeting the real felt needs of people, it is by-passed with little feeling of bad conscience. Another way of saying this is that organization must always follow function, and not vice versa.

The second general observation is that an organization can never be a substitute for involved, concerned and highly motivated people who trust each other and who are willing to work with each other. One of the questions that the experience of the Metropolitan Area Church Board raises is how large an organization can become before the inter-personal relationships and trust are violated. It seems as though the inter-personal relationships of the core group were the creative driving force that gave rise to the Metropolitan Area Church Board, as well as to many other of the organizations. Yet when these organizations come to the place where organizational hierarchy, constitutions, by-laws, etc., are substituted for that informal creativity, the organization begins to change. This leads to a generalization; *the role and function of persons in the organization is probably different at different points in the life cycle of that organization.* That is, in the beginning of an organization, the role of leadership is to build the creative myth that can catch the imagination of people.

Second, it can be observed that the ecumenical organizations in Columbus generally suffer from the lack of understanding about the pluralistic nature of both society and of the Church. There is apparently no clear understanding that only out of functional differentiation can there be real unity. The myth seems to prevail that what we are about is building uniformity. The second observation that can be made is that there is no clear understanding about the inter-relationship between the various functional levels in the life of the community and in the life of the Church. Those who function at the grass-roots level believe that "if it ain't local, it ain't real." Those who function at the neighborhood or metropolitan level seem to have a lack of sensitivity to those levels in the life of the community and Church which are below them, as well as those levels which are above them.

Third, there seems to be an impediment to ecumenical life due from the myth which prevails in our society about social contract. This myth has given rise to traditional constitutions, by-laws, etc. The need seems to be for openness and flexibility based upon informal covenant as the basis of trust and mutual commitment. And yet at the same time there is conflict with those who think that the purely contractual constitutional and by-law basis is the only valid means of functioning.

The final methodological and mythological factor which seems to emerge is that we do not know how to link the resources of wealthy congregations, people and institutions to the needs of those who have few resources without impugning the integrity of those with needs through paternalism.

By and large, the greatest category of impediment for ecumenical involvement has to do with institutional factors. The first of these has to do with the inertia which involves institutional allegiances to styles of life and ministry that are no longer very functional in the contemporary world. Further, allegiances to canon law and legal motifs which developed at another time in the life and history of the Church now appear to be impeding the freedom which we need for creativity in ecumenical relations among the denominations. Finally, the inertia of history is evident in that priority decisions of ten, fifteen or twenty years ago still obligate the Church. Examples of these are the large buildings which have long-term mortgages, the priority for camping and/or Christian education, homes for the aged, hospitals, etc., all of which claim a high proportion of our available resources. They were once priorities in the life of the Church, but are now less important.

Still another institutional factor has to do with the organizational crisis. Many of the traditional Church organizations are now at the point in their organizational life cycle where they are nearing crystallization and potential institutional death. Because of lack of vitality and affirmation of previous societal values, they are a negative witness to the on-going life and work of the Church. They are absorbing a phenomenal amount of resources and producing very little noticeable results for any large number of persons. Further, we find that frequently the wrong prescription is being given to those denominational and ecumenical organizations. For instance, it is not usually enough to prescribe to a floundering organization the antidote of building new goals and objectives. Goals and objectives are only useful to an organization which already has flexibility and objectivity, but which needs a means of focusing its energies.

Closely related to this is the crisis of leadership and leadership styles. Many professional Church leaders were trained in the "Herr Pastor" motif, i.e., he was trained to be "the parson," or "the person." With a society which is moving away from hierarchy and toward an egalitarian style of leadership, this causes real difficulty in terms of creative leadership. Further, the crisis of leadership is intensified because of the high mobility of leaders in the life of the Church. Most ecumenical organizations are continually experiencing the "floating crap game." Because of transfers from one assignment to another, the leaders that you work with in any geographical "turf" or ecumenical project will normally change significantly from year to year. Continuity is very difficult to maintain. It is difficult to maintain the creative nucleus that you need for creative on-going ecumenical involvement.

Another institutional impediment seems to relate to the inherent need for pragmatic experience to emerge into common celebration. The denominations have jealously protected the sacraments and other motifs of celebration. When an ecumenical group has worked together and experienced unity and community, but the members are unable to celebrate that in the fullness of their understanding through the utilization of sacraments, etc., they are impeded in their vitality and in a fundamental need for fulfillment. The interaction and openness which is common to the ecumenical experience is somehow falsely violated by the intrusion of sanctions, rules and regulations.

Still another kind of impediment to ecumenical life and mission has to do with denominationalism. By denominationalism we mean the denomination first and the Church second, i.e., misconstrued priorities. There seems to be a very great feeling of "we" and "they"—we being the denomination, they being the ecumenical appendage. There is evidence on many occasions of a significant lack of candor between denominations. Some denominations are saying *yes* to ecumenical proposals when they are in council with other denominations, but when they are closeted in their own council, they are making decisions which, in fact, do not back up the commitments they made ecumenically. There is also an inherent kind of conservatism within the denominations. One person indicated that "denominationalism is the conspiracy of the hierarchy against the laity." Another said that "the denomination is the figment of the hierarchy's imagination which had no reality at the grass-roots level." Although these statements are extreme, they do indicate something of the problems that extreme denominationalism causes. The *apparent generalization is that the larger the numerical base of the denomination in a given area, the more difficult it is to work with on an ecumenical basis.*

The final institutional impediment has to do with the matter of resources. Ecumenical agencies are at the second or third level of allocation from the constituency, which means they receive leftover funds. For example, a neighborhood council of churches only receives money for its operation after the needs of the local parish and denominational askings are met, and a metropolitan level ecumenical institution receives monetary resources only after the needs of the congregation and the judicatory are met.

2.4.2 *External Impediments*

Closely related to the mythological and methodological difficulties described above are the external cultural expectations of ecumenism. The image of ecumenism is that it is trying to develop a superchurch with centralized control and common faith. This threatens persons who find real validity in the uniqueness of their denominational and local myth and jeopardizes their desire to retain authority at the lowest possible level. This puts ecumenism in direct conflict with many of the prevalent tenets of the culture of which the participants are a part.

Second, ecumenism which is dealing with diversity in the Church and pluralism in society must learn how to use conflict creatively. The whole mood of our culture is to avoid conflict at all cost.

The third cultural factor that seems to impede ecumenism has to do with the expectation that the Church is to deal with the individual and not with the corporate problems of society. Whenever the churches become involved in corporate problems of society, tension emerges.

2.5 *Ecclesiological and Organizational Implications*

The above data have many implications for ecclesiological and organizational style. There are at least four principal implications. The first of these has to do with ecclesiological issues of authority vs. freedom and control vs. flexibility. Some denominations are obviously threatened by that which they cannot control. They tend to control that which threatens them through sanctions or provide little or no resources for the ecumenical enterprise. This is a closed stance. It causes deviation. It forces creativity outside. It tries to preserve the status quo. Yet, the denomination's very life may well depend upon an openness toward other denominational styles and innovative styles of life and mission which are being developed through ecumenical interaction.

The second observation is that pluriform style will be essential for the continued viability and life of the Church in a pluralistic culture. No one denomination has adequate resources or traditions to develop the full range of styles that are needed to meet the diverse needs of people. Only by building a plan of complementary diversity can the necessary pluriform interrelated style be developed.

The third general concern has to do with the emerging leadership styles. The whole role of hierarchy (pyramid) is changing. Authority is shared. It is a privilege accorded by the group. It is given to those who are trusted in order to facilitate the group's fulfillment and purpose.

The fourth factor has to do with the understanding of the functions of various levels in the life of a community. The metropolitan level is not a higher level than the local level. Both are essential, and there must be an interactive style and pattern developed so that the metropolitan level of concerns can interact with the local levels of concern, to the mutual synergistic benefit of all.

2.6 *Theological Implications*

At least five theological themes emerged from the Columbus experience which need to be developed in more detail and depth. Some of these are not central themes of normal Faith and Order dialogue. The first of these has to do with the theology of creation. The experience in Columbus as a community would indicate that creation is in fact a process and God is the Creative Being, and his purposes are creative and redemptive. It is also evident that the nature of creation requires order—the opposite, anti-creation or chaos, is sin. Finally, it is apparent that mankind is endowed with freedom which allows each individual by choice to participate in the anti-creation or the creative process.

A second general area of theological implication from the Columbus experience develops around institutions as a means and not as an end. Religious social systems or institutions are the vehicles by which people are nurtured in their allegiance toward active participation in creation. And, finally, the theological assumption is that religious institutions are the means by which these people demonstrate feasibility of participations in the on-going creation process at all levels of civilization. Therefore, the purpose of the religious institution we call the Church, both as a people and as an institution, is to move the social system and ultimately the civilization toward participation in creation as opposed to anti-creation.

The final observation is that ecclesiological and organizational factors are significantly modified by the interaction of values, beliefs, ideology, dogma, etc., the point at which the organization stands in its life cycle and the current historical context.

3.0 *Community*

Community is an important variable in the shape of the unity we seek both as an internal factor within the Church and as an external factor. The way we understand these two dimensions of community has significant implications for ecclesiology.

3.1 *The Community Around Us*

The sociological understanding of community revolves around such ideas as complementary diversity of function (although not necessarily self-sustaining), mutuality, boundaries and sanction, or control. Traditionally these have been described in horizontal or spatial terms. This is valid, but it is obvious that communities of interest are also emerging on a vertical basis.

3.1.1 *Horizontal Communities*

Society organizes its life into functional levels. The simplest of these is the neighborhood. Institutions and institutional arrangements of our society begin from the bottom-up rather than from the top-down. That is, all institutions begin first of all because persons have basic human needs which must be met. Those who are experiencing these common needs have two alternatives. They can compete with each other to meet their needs, or they can develop patterns of cooperation. In the latter there is a tendency to associate with others with similar needs for the purpose of meeting mutual needs. This results in the formation of informal associations. If the informal association succeeds in meeting the basic human needs of a segment of society, then that informal association will be organized into a more formal institutional structure. These more formal institutional structures would be equivalent, in most cases, to our local churches. They normally exist at a neighborhood level.

In the complexity of an urbanized technological society, it soon becomes apparent that there are support functions which must be provided if that local institution is to effectively provide for the needs of its constituents. This usually results in some kind of an association of these local institutions. Internally this association of local institutions functions essentially as a support system to provide certain specialization and resource material functions which are not economically feasible locally. Externally it functions in behalf of all of the local institutions to deal with the problems and issues that are common to all of these groups in the larger community. Still a third level of institutional formation takes place when these community associations band together at a regional, state or even larger level to provide still more specialized internal and external functions in behalf of their constituents. Other levels are also identifiable and often emerge to provide some kind of overall coordination and impact at even national and world levels.

These observations indicate that the fundamental functioning of our society goes on largely at horizontal levels. The vertical bureaucratic structures, in theory, function to link these horizontal levels together. This linkage is essentially a function of communication, and each of the levels in the ascending hierarchy of levels essentially functions as a more highly specialized support system for the lower levels. The economy of scale dictates that as the need for a functional specialty increases, the base of constituents must also increase.

These general observations of institutional formation and the increasing specialization of function within a given institutional system level, as you move from the grass-roots to other higher hierarchical functional levels, give rise to some empirical observations that these horizontal functional levels have geographic (spatial) implications. The following may provide a model of functional institutional level and their geographic implication.

The "A" Level

In the rural society this level would be the neighborhood. In an urban society it would be the sub-neighborhood level—perhaps an apartment complex, two or three square blocks or a grade school district. In other cases in the urban setting, it might be based upon interests as opposed to geographical considerations. Basically this level is the level at which day to day human interaction takes place. Communication at this level is generally limited to informal word of mouth.

The "B" Level

(This level would contain two or more "A" levels.) In the rural setting this level would be a hamlet or a village and its immediate surrounding area. In the urban setting it would be an urban neighborhood. This level would provide for the more sophisticated exchange of goods and services. It would provide for a relatively full range of religious institutions of the various denominations so that a relatively broad range of human religious needs can be met. It would provide some employment opportunities and perhaps a weekly newspaper to provide basic communication within that functional level.

The "C" Level

(Comprised of two or more "B" levels.) In the urban setting this level might be composed of two or more urban neighborhoods known, for example, as the West Side, the East Side or the core city. In the rural setting it would functionally be similar to the county seat town. Distributed across this level is a higher degree of specialization which functions for the needs of a much broader population. This level would provide many employment opportunities and export as well as import products. In terms of communication this level would frequently have its own newspaper, sometimes on a daily basis, and its own radio station.

The "D" Level

(Comprised of two or more "C" levels.) This level is the one that sociologists, social geographers and economists call the "functional area" level. In the midwestern states, it is a city like Fort Wayne, Lima, Carbondale or Bloomington and its hinterland. Essentially this level is made up of an urban growth center and its rural hinterland. In the midwest, it tends to be a geographic area which is approximately sixty miles in diameter. It is a delicately balanced social-economic entity providing goods and services which can be exchanged with other similar functional areas, as well as providing goods and services for its own constituency. This level has a broad enough population base that communication is multi-media. It has television stations, daily newspapers and strong radio stations. Here you would also normally find a four-year college and a full range of religious functions, ranging from the one-room church to the cathedral.

In a large metropolitan center like the Boston SMSA this level would compare to the corporate city of Boston.

The "E" Level

(Comprised of two or more "D" levels.) This level of human economic community is made up of cities like Indianapolis, St. Louis, Minneapolis-St. Paul, Madison, and their hinterlands of influence. It is frequently called the regional level. This scale provides increased specialization. These cities tend to be centers for state government, have minor federal offices, and are influential in wholesale, trade and financial functions. Internally they possess resources to meet basic day-to-day, weekly, monthly, and annual needs of persons within a rather large geographic area.

In the larger metropolitan areas such as Cleveland, Ohio, for in-

The Imbedding of Societal Functional Levels

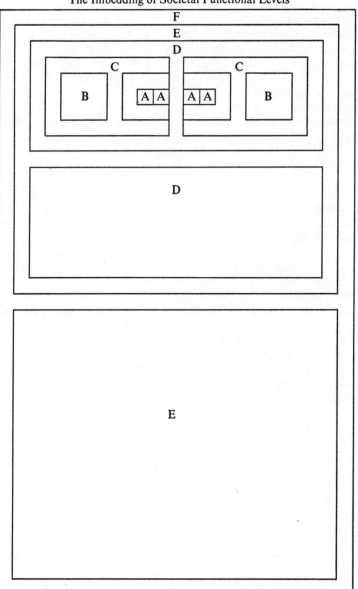

stance, this level would roughly correspond to the corporate city of Cleveland and its immediate suburbs.

The "F" Level

(Comprised of two or more "E" levels.) This level is the national "divisional" level of our society. Cities like Chicago, Atlanta, Los Angeles, Dallas-Fort Worth and Boston provide a level of specialization which serves a whole cultural segment or division of the nation. At this level are found the principal federal offices of H.E.W., H.U.D., U.S.D.A., etc. It is at this level that you also find the principal intersection of transportation with important airports, rail yards, and intersecting freeways. The telephone, radio and television communication networks have principal intersections here. The production of goods, and financial institutions which provide services for a whole segment of the nation, intersect here. Also located in these centers is a very high level of specialty among the legal, economic, medical and scientific fields. The national sub-culture is important to the understanding of this scale of society. That is, that divisional area of the nation to which the city of Chicago relates is generally represented by the mid-western "mind set"; that area which relates to Atlanta tends to hold a common value structure that has its roots in the historic southern society; that area which relates to the city of Boston is typified by a cultural pattern which has its roots in historic New England; and that area which is related to Dallas-Fort Worth is typified by a cultural pattern and value structure which is related to a life style developed on the open plains.

It is at these levels that culturally identifiable styles of religion are also evident.

The "G" Level

(Comprised of two or more "F" levels.) This level of societal organizations is essentially equivalent to the national functional level. Two or three cities in our nation typify this level. Washington, D.C. functions nationally for political concerns, New York City functions nationally for communication and economic or financial concerns, and Boston tends to function as the national level educational center. This is the level where national policy is made, resources are gathered, and allocations in terms of resource distribution are made for our society. It is also the level at which major communication functions intersect for the whole nation.

These functional levels tend to relate to each other in a hierarchical functional manner. The hierarchical institutional function can be defined in the following way: "A" is related to "B" as "AB" is related to "C" as "ABC" is related to "D", etc. It is an ascending scale of function of institutions. The concept is based on progressive inclusiveness from the least to the most complex institutional social system. Take the economic systems as an example. At the B level a branch bank would be a normal occurrence. At the C and D levels there would be large banks which provide all of the functions traditional to the B, C and D levels, but which also provide correspondent banking functions, i.e., loan money to smaller banks. At the divisional level you would find federal banks which serve the correspondent banks throughout that whole division of the nation. At the national level such as New York City, you will find banks of national and international prominence which provide for services ranging all the way from the services of the neighborhood branch bank to the national and international needs. This is the example of hierarchy of function.

Summary

The A level of society is the simplest level of the social system. Most informal needs can be met at that level. Each succeeding level of society is increasingly more complex because it is a system of highly specialized systems. Thus, each level is increasingly more specialized, yet in reality these higher levels exist to provide support functions for the levels below. This has implications for patterns of participation also. At the A level a high percentage of the persons who live at that level can be, and are, involved in its day-to-day operation. Some of those persons because of need and skill are able to participate at the B or C level. However, by the time you reach the national level the percentage of the total population which is capable of, or interested in, participating declines significantly. In a very real sense these levels are operated by professional specialists.

3.1.2 *Vertical Communities*

Beginning with the emergence of craftsmen's guilds in the Renaissance, man has increasingly organized his life around interests and current issues which cut vertically across the horizontal communities. These interact with the horizontal communities, but they are specialized communities in terms of interest and function.

In some ways some ecumenical organizations resemble a vertically organized community of religious persons. They have their roots in a horizontal community, but because of openness, world view and common perception of the issues of life, they become a community of interest and advocacy.

3.1.3 *Observation About Community*

Alfred Whitehead once said, "The major advances of civilization are processes which all but wreck the society in which they occur." Perhaps the greatest wreckage that the recent flood-tide of progress has cast upon the beach is our sense of community. This was first noted and poignantly expressed by the sociologist, Robert A. Nisbet in his celebrated work *The Quest for Community.* Man has paid dearly for his breathtaking leap into freedom, and now he realizes it. "Not the free individual, but the lost in-dividual—not independence, but isolation—not self-discovery, but self-ob-session—not conqueror, but to be conquered." These are the major states of mind in contemporary imaginative literature. The question is whether the new open styles of institutions which we are generally developing can creatively fulfill man's quest for community.

As you follow a path of social evolution up to the present time, you find very few models of a type of community that modern man believes he has lost. The medieval city, the European rural village, and the small early American town fall far short of living up to the glowing pictures so often painted of them. They did provide a sense of community, but they did so at a fearful cost. Conformity, hierarchy, lack of privacy and the sheer dreariness are only some of the price tags that the sense of community has traditionally borne.

The fact is that modern Western man cannot tolerate a community in the traditional sense. He is much too liberated, or, if you prefer, much too spoiled. He has become too devoted to such things as independence, pri-vacy, and variety. He requires something new. What is the new? The basis of community is not simple residence, but mutual or interrelated activity. Ortega y Gasset once pointed out that "people do not live together merely to be together." Consequently, the rudimentary ecumenical organization which we saw in Columbus started out by fulfilling this primary purpose of community. The ecumenical organizations in Columbus which seeming-ly have succeeded are those which have moved to fulfill the emotional, the physical, the financial, and the intellectual needs of those who put a stake in the life of these small communities.

3.2 *The Community of Faith*

In many of their dimensions the parish churches in Columbus have only one factor in common. That revolves around faith and tradition. This is to say that the majority tend not to be geographic parishes. The majori-ty of Protestant churches in Old Columbus are truly gathered, not in the historic sense, but in the sense that they represent the home community from which the congregational participants moved. They retain membership in the old church, but actually live someplace else. This pattern is also emerging in Catholic churches.

If the community of faith is a prototype community which provides means to demonstrate wholeness, justice and reconciliation, then the current style of congregational organization may be less than the best in the contemporary historical setting. This has a full range of implications. Worship and sacrament are means by which we celebrate our oneness and wholeness with each other, as well as our common participation in the purposes of creation. Elements of the creation become the means by which the community symbolically celebrates the mysteries of that which they have been and that which they are doing together. Yet, for many in the pluralistic culture, the congregation is an unreal community, and by the criteria suggested above there is nothing to celebrate. There is the individual doing private acts of worship with little sense of community to celebrate.

It was evident in Columbus that one of the most pressing theological and ecclesiological issues has to do with community. What is it? What kinds of organizational style will give it symbolic meaning? How do we move from institutional means rooted in the past to new organizational styles more appropriate to the present without violating the integrity of experience developed in the past? Equally important, how, given all the historic divisions rooted in the past, can Christians of different traditions celebrate their oneness when they do experience it in ecumenical activities without violating the sacramental constraints of those traditions? In fact, with the current move toward openness and flexibility, it was evident in Columbus that pragmatic need is transcending historical formulations and traditions. Pragmatically the need for community seems to be transcending the ethnic and social sources of denominationalism and the resulting difference in practice.

4.0 Leadership and Organizational Style

Time was when the pyramidal system of leadership functioned well. There are three themes which emerge in the Columbus experience that give clues as to the future shape of leadership. The first of these is related to authority, the second relates to collegiality of leadership and decision-making, and the third has to do with patterning for action.

4.1 Authority

Many of the theological definitions of ecclesiological authority are rooted in a three-tiered universe and a monarchical and prime minister view of societal organization. The ecumenical experience in Columbus seems to be challenging these views.

For some time sociology has observed that there are two kinds of leadership. The first is the enacted leader. Essentially he possesses specialized skills and leads because of his position and skill. A teacher in the public school and a parish pastor are examples. The second kind of leader is the "crescive" or the leader who emerges out of the group. He is the person who is accorded the privilege of leadership. He is slightly ahead of the group and represents a direction for the group, but is not so far ahead as to have lost the confidence of the group.

Observation in Columbus would lead to the conclusion that still a third dynamic is at work in leadership styles. In part, it is the product of a different concept of reality, which sees an interacting universe rather than the three-story universe. This leads to a more egalitarian view of man. Related to this pattern is the fact that equality of education and the broadening of the middle class have equipped more persons for participation in both decision-making and leadership. This means that people at each level in the life of the Church are making their own decisions rather than taking direction from other levels. The task of ecumenism therefore becomes one of linkage so that patterns of creative interaction can emerge. This means that no one group or person is in charge. What happens is less manipulatable by the few. Furthermore, authority in the traditional sense is ignored or bypassed. If the proposed action is authentic to the experience of the group, there is little need felt to check with anyone else.

This stance finds itself in direct conflict with the orderly and approved ecclesiastical traditions and laws which have their origin in another historical context. From a traditional perspective the emerging pattern resembles anarchy and chaos. Yet, from an interaction perspective, the emerging style has potential for real participatory democracy and wholeness.

4.2 *Collegiality*

These observations about emerging decision-making and leadership styles mean that true collegiality is beginning to emerge in Columbus. The distance between pastor and parishioner is breaking down. The distance between ecclesiastical leadership and constituency is breaking down. Status is not as important as it once was. Persons are accepted for what they are and what they can contribute to the whole group.

Thus, leadership is increasingly shared. Goals are set out of the group's needs and perceptions of the community's issues. Group members, regardless of status, work in task group style to implement those goals which they pragmatically feel to be the priorities. Each task group's accountability is to the whole group, rather than to a person. This means that the leadership role of the enacted leader is increasingly that of facilitator and enabler, rather than accountable administrator. It also means that sacramental roles are changing. The clergyman no longer stands as the channel of grace between his people and the Creator. Rather, he stands with the people. Together they participate in the on-going creation.

This stance also means that younger clergymen are entering into team relationships with their peers more easily than did their predecessors. As they experience the mutual support and fulfillment of team relationships, they will expect their ecclesiastical leadership to function accordingly. This team relationship is evident already in some of the Columbus neighborhood clusters. Collegiality is beginning to function in ecumenical and denominational decision-making. It will probably be the wave of the future.

4.3 Leadership Patterning

These trends mean that leadership is patterning in styles which were unknown in the past. This patterning is occurring in at least three arenas. The first has to do with the creative minority. In Columbus, nearly all of the ecumenical organizations are the product of a creative minority of persons who came together because of common concerns and discussed the concerns long enough to enable them to learn to trust each other; finally this gave rise to an organization which can respond to the need which they felt in common. It was discovered in Columbus that in only a few cases had an ecumenical organization been organized because someone at the metropolitan level felt that people who lived or worshiped in a certain geographic area should work together. Self-interest which interacts with the self-interest of others can lead to creativity and trust. It is difficult to generate this from the outside.

The second patterning of leadership identified in Columbus has to do with changing and dynamic coalition task forces. These are people who for one reason or another come together around an issue and work until it is solved. They then disband to reconfigure around other issues. Apparently, these persons work in a tertiary relationship with the creative minority. They are not controlled by the minority, but they respond only to those issues which converge with their self-interest, work until there is a solution, and then disband. This pattern was apparent in Columbus in the neighborhood clusters and also in the Metropolitan Area Church Board approach to welfare reform.

Patterning is occurring in still a third way. It relates to peer groupings of enacted leaders. People of similar background and responsibility seem to feel most comfortable together. Thus bishops are beginning to relate to each other, as are middle judicatory executives, downtown pastors, and neighborhood pastors. Each group is increasingly generating concerns. The ecumenical task is to link these.

Summary

All of this means that the styles by which organizations make their decisions, order their life and do their work are changing significantly. The representative principle is giving way to a participatory and negotiation style that requires the creative management of conflict. Interaction is being increased. Openness and flexibility is to facilitate and enable rather than to direct. Out of this common life, the community can authentically celebrate its oneness and its common purpose in creation.

5.0 *Toward the Shape of the Unity We Seek*

The shape of the unity we seek will be forged largely from the bottom-up. This is not to say that there is nothing for the higher judicatories to do, but it is to say that it is more difficult for creativity to emerge in the higher judicatories because many of their tasks are maintenance-oriented. The lesson which the judicatory needs to learn is how to recognize local creativity, not get in its way, and to link it with other creative experiences in such a way that unity can emerge. This is a process. The judicatory must learn how to facilitate it. This will only happen if two criteria are met. First, the judicatory must have some sense of a vision about the future of the Church. These dreams or models serve to motivate. They become a self-fulfilling prophecy. Second, there are some marks of the future shape of the Church which can serve as criteria for evaluation of the alternative creative thrusts.

5.1 *The Marks of the Shape of the Unity We Seek*

1. *Movement from the Tolerance Typical of Denominationalism to the Trust Necessary for Ecumenicity.*
2. *Freedom of Experimentation.*
3. *Flexibility and Diversity.*
4. *The Corporate Ability To Speak and Act Prophetically.*
5. *Reorientation of Values.* Functionally, society expects the Church to conserve values. The new structure of the Church must become more discriminating in the values it conserves, because not all values enhance the prophetic message of the Church. The Church must consciously

conserve those values which will enhance its striving toward ecumenicity. The new forms of the Church, therefore, must specialize in conserving only values, beliefs and practices that will accomplish its divine imperative.

6. *New Ethos.* The structural form of the Church must be such that a new vitality will become integral in the tone of communication, in the expression of beliefs and in the sense of mission. This understanding must pervade the immediate tasks and the ultimate goals of the Church. The ceremonies and rituals will need to take on this new vitality. This may mean serious revision of many of the rituals and ceremonies because they frequently communicate memories that are divisive rather than unifying in their result.

7. *Self-Analytical—Divesting.* The emerging structure will have built-in processes for evaluation and adjustment. It must be its own worst critic. It must raise and deal with basic questions about its basic institutionalism. Mass society may well demand that for the sake of flexibility the institutional manifestation of the Church divest itself of all "institutional crutches and excess baggage."

5.2 *The Ecclesiological System*

The ecclesiological system is comprised of several interacting parts which make it possible for people to meet the ultimate value questions of life and death, both at the individual and the corporate levels. Increasingly this must deal with the pluralistic context. All systems have a minimum of three interacting parts. These are: input, core coordination (maintenance functions) and output. This system should provide means for the above-listed marks of the shape of the unity we seek to be realized.

5.2.1 *The Components of the Ecclesiological System*

5.2.1.1 *The Input Components.* These include: the congregations and their constituency; the neighborhood parish or cluster groupings as described above; the metropolitan or area coalitions, consortia; the ecumenical agencies; and the pluralism represented in denominational traditions, and the diversity represented by racial, ethnic and regional value orientations.

5.2.1.2 *The Core Components.* These components are at the heart of the system. Its interacting functions include: a process for receiving the input, interacting around it, prioritizing, strategizing and implementing; and the support services to enhance and maintain the process. These usually in-

THE THEORETICAL ECCLESIOLOGICAL SYSTEM

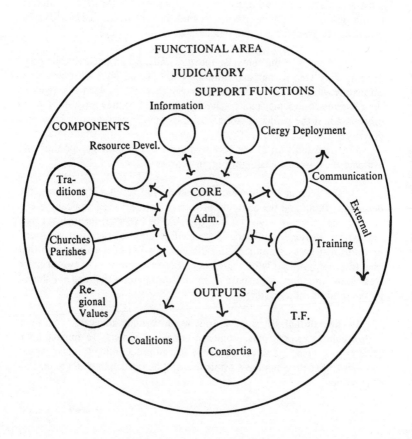

clude such things as: ecclesiastical control mechanisms to sanction the clergy, planning and research functions, resource multiplication and development, administration, internal and external communication and interpretation, training, and information storage and retrieval.

The core component need not own all these support systems, but it must have access to them. This component of the ecclesiological system must be able to facilitate decisions or at least enable the diverse interests of the pluralistic religious system to find their common needs and agendas, coelesce around them and pursue them.

As indicated in the remarks above, it must be an open flexible component. This means that accountability is "played out" in a new way. Sometimes it only provides the arena whereby like-minded segments of the religious community can do that which they feel they must do. On the other hand, at the points of consensus, the core component may have programs to "call its own."

The final function of the core component is to manage, monitor and evaluate the implementation or output process.

5.2.1.3 *The Output Component.* Output is the result of the input, the decision-making and the enabling processes. In the ecclesiological system, at least the following styles of output could be expected through the system which provided the input. First, configuration of task forces around issues of concerns common to the life and mission of the Church in that area (diocese, presbytery or conference). Second, consortia of two or more traditional groupings who share common self-interests that are not shared by the total religious system.

In the external arena the output would include advocacy, coalitions with secular groups around common concerns, projects to impact upon societal problems, and the evangelistic task of proclaiming to persons that through Christ they can have wholeness and be participants in the destiny of creation.

Arleon L. Kelley

A Value, Role, Institutional Life Cycle Interaction Model

Arleon L. Kelley

Formal Ideology

| Rational | Emotional |

Dysfunctional Goals and Action Anomie → Alienation or Dysfunctional Myth

Descending Institution

Ascending Institution

No doubt

Flexible operational

Ethical

Absolute

Stubborn Continuance

Accelerating Loss

The Crucial Third (Radical Change Necessary)

The Fatal Third (If Negative Close)

Reactionary (system as an end)

Revolutionary (values as an end)

Rehabilitation (past systems then values)

Conservative (past values, then systems)

Dominant Roles In Static Institutions

Intermediate Plateaus

The Decisive Third (Minor Adjustments Needed)

Synthesizes (past-present) future)

Pragmatic (present) oriented)

Intuitive (future oriented)

Feeling (past oriented)

Dominant Roles In Dynamic Institutions

Membership Plateau (A Fluctuating but Sustained Average)

Increasing Growth (Christian witness wins Community Confidence)

Demonstrating Life (A Vital Christian Witness)

Accelerating Growth

Interacting Constituency and Leadership Roles

Effective ← Action

Goals

Dream

Fantasy

Functional Myth

Effective

Rational

Emotional

Informal Beliefs

The Shape of the Unity We Seek in Worship

The major features of the shape of the unity we seek in worship are: (1) a plurality of forms of worship, (2) recognition of all these forms as valid, (3) new communities of worship, (4) active participation of all, and (5) integrity of Christian worship. An explanation of these features follows.

1. *A Plurality of Forms of Worship*

By "plurality of forms" we do not mean simply various services of worship such as baptism, Eucharist, confirmation, proclamation of the Word, morning prayer, etc. Assuming these, we intend primarily a variety of forms resulting from different experiences and understandings of Christian faith.

Thus there will be forms of worship reflecting the Roman Catholic tradition, the Presbyterian-Reformed tradition, and other Christian traditions, both Eastern and Western. Perhaps there will be some forms expressive of the common elements of our diverse experiences and understandings. Certainly there will be new forms[1] of worship expressing a new experience of Christian faith in its encounter with secularized, technological culture; a new understanding of the Church as God's people within the world, sharing its struggles and aspirations, and heralding the coming of God's reign; and new awareness of the unity of all Christians, despite denominational divisions.

Such a plurality of forms of worship is justifiably expected. The New Testament bears witness to slightly different forms of eucharistic celebration.[2] Free prayer seems to have been especially vigorous in Pauline churches.[3] Whatever the New Testament evidence, the history of the Church provides ample witness to a multiplicity of liturgies. Theology testifies that this plurality of forms serves to bring out the richness of God's revelation in Jesus Christ, facilitates appropriation of revelation through faith by men and women of diverse cultures, and enables men and women to express their faith in worship suited to their mentality and needs.

2. *Recognition of All These Forms as Valid*

In contrast to the present situation, these many forms of worship will be distinguished by their official and popular recognition by all the churches and their members as (1) legitimate expressions of Christian faith and worship, (2) grounded in mutually recognized ministries, (3) efficacious for salvation, (4) satisfying denominational obligations and expectations, and (5) possible fulfillments of personal needs. An explanation follows.

Recognition of the many forms of worship will be *official*, that is, explicitly and formally stated by the competent overseeing persons or bodies of each of the churches, so that there will be no question in the minds of the members of any Church about the worth of the worship of any other Church. Recognition will also be *popular*, that is, the members of all churches, clerical and lay, will acknowledge and respect the value of the worship of every Church and feel free to participate in it.

Acceptance will extend to the many forms of worship as *legitimate expressions* of *faith by which (fides qua)* we trust in Jesus and *faith which* or *about which (fides quae)* we affirm trust in Jesus. For further clarification of this distinction and its implications, see the section of this statement on the shape of the unity we seek in belief. That section also offers grounds for the possibility of this recognition.

Authentic Christian worship presupposes "the reality of ministry and priesthood of Word and sacraments as having their source in the Spirit and the risen Lord."[4] Lack of mutual recognition of this reality by the churches vis-à-vis one another has been and continues to be a major source of separation in worship. For these reasons, official and popular recognition will extend to the many forms of worship as grounded in mutually *recognized ministries*. For the possibility of this mutual acceptance, see the statement *Ministry in the Church* of this consultation,[5] and also *Reconsiderations* by this consultation,[6] and Kilian McDonnell's "Ways of Validating Ministry."[7]

The many forms of worship will be recognized as *efficacious for salvation*, in contrast to the centuries-long doubt, suspicion, and even denial of the efficacy of various Christian churches' worship. The possibility of this recognition is demonstrated by its partial realization, for example, among the various churches in the Presbyterian-Reformed tradition, and in Vatican II's statement: "The brethren divided from us also carry out many of the sacred actions of the Christian religion. Undoubtedly, in ways that vary according to the conditions of each Church or community, these actions can truly engender a life of grace, and can be rightly described as capable of providing access to the community of salvation."[8]

A current obstacle to worship together is the sense of obligation which Christians feel to participate in their own denominations' worship. This feeling may arise from respect for the legislation of one's Church, from loyalty to one's own Church, or from suspicion of other churches' worship. In the unity we seek in worship, this narrow sense of obligation will no longer exist because the churches will recognize officially and popularly the many forms of Christian worship as *satisfying obligations and expectations* which may arise from belonging to one or another denomination. The possibility of this recognition lies in the previous acknowledgments and in a new understanding of the Church which cuts through denominational divisions and is articulated in this statement's section on the unity we seek in the Church as the people of God.

Acceptance of the many forms of worship as *possible fulfillment of personal needs* will indicate a basis on which a person may choose the worship he or she will participate in. For example, because a person needs a supporting community for his or her Christian life, he or she will usually share in a particular community's worship. But because he or she feels the need to celebrate with a friend on the occasion of the latter's wedding, he or she will participate fully in the worship of another community on that day. The possibility of this recognition is manifested in most churches' acknowledging the right of their members to participate in the worship of other churches as they see fit. Even the Roman Catholic Church, generally reserved in this matter, permits and even encourages its members to participate, under certain conditions, in the worship of Eastern Orthodox Churches to satisfy a variety of personal needs.[9]

3. *New Communities of Worship*

The worship in the unity we seek will sometimes be celebrated, not by denominational congregations, but by groups of Christians from several denominations who experience together in a special way Christian *kerygma* (proclamation), *diakonia* (service), and *koinonia* (fellowship) and the desire to express and nourish this experience in worship. Obviously these groups will not be territorial parishes of any particular denomination. The possibility of such communities flows from the recognition of many forms of worship which we have just described, and from what is proposed about the people of God, unity in belief, and cooperative organization in other sections of this statement.

4. *Active Participation*

For a developed explanation of this feature, see the exploratory paper, "Toward the Unity We Seek in Worship," by a subcommittee of this consultation.[10] Here it is sufficient to point out that this active participation extends beyond the actual celebration of worship to include the planning of the manner in which received forms of worship will be celebrated and the creation of new forms of worship. Participation to this extent, involving laity as well as clergy, women as well as men, young and old, and other groups hitherto excluded from a say in the form of their own worship, will result in forms of worship more clearly related to Christian life and mission in the world, and more expressive of the equality of all in Christ, regardless of sex, race, ethnic background, social or ecclesiastical status, and so forth. The possibility of such participation is evident in the steps which various churches have taken in recent years in this direction, in accord with growing awareness of the Church as the people of God, all members sharing in some way in the priesthood of Jesus Christ.

5. *Integrity of Christian Worship*

Naturally we expect the worship we seek in unity to possess those qualities which will make it authentically Christian and effective for Christian life and mission. Thus the worship we seek will be characterized not only by the active participation of all but also by a combination of structure and freedom, an involvement of the whole person, a sense of transcendence, an orientation to mission, a balance of Word and sacraments, and a shared understanding of Christian worship. These characteristics are explained in detail in the paper "Toward the Unity We Seek in Worship" mentioned above.

* * * * *

The data gathered about the Columbus ecumenical activity indicate the need for a plurality of forms of worship. "It can be observed that the ecumenical organizations in Columbus generally suffer from the lack of understanding about the pluralistic nature of both society and of the Church."[11] An external impediment to ecumenism is "the image of ecumenism . . . that it is trying to develop a superchurch with centralized control and common faith. This threatens people who find real validity in the uniqueness of their denominational and local myth."[12] This plurality of forms will include developments of traditional forms and new forms, for the Columbus data indicate that religious institutions have a life cycle and at a certain stage tend to become dysfunctional unless changed.[13] Moreover, "the ceremonies and rituals will need to take on this new vitality [of the unity we seek]. This may mean serious revision of many of the rituals and ceremonies because they frequently communicate memories that are divisive rather than unifying in their result."[14]

Lack of recognition is the negative result of the belief that one's own church has everything necessary for salvation and that members must be protected from the dubious offerings of other churches. The data in Columbus indicate that "another institutional impediment seems to be related to the inherent need for pragmatic experience to emerge into common celebration. The denominations have jealously protected the sacraments and other motifs of celebration. When an ecumenical group has worked together and experienced unity and community, but its members are unable to celebrate that in the fullness of their understanding through the utilization of sacraments, etc., they are impeded in their vitality and in a fundamental need for fulfillment. The interaction and openness which is common to the ecumenical experience is somehow falsely violated by the intrusion of sanctions, rules, and regulations."[15] "By and large, the greatest category of impediment for ecumenical involvement has to do with institutional factors. . . . Allegiances to canon law and legal motifs which developed at another time in the life and history of the Church now appear to be impeding the freedom which we need for creativity in ecumenical relations among the denominations."[16] This impediment is most felt in regard to mutual acceptance of the Eucharist and ministries.[17]

As for new communities of worship, "the basis of community is not simple residence, but mutual or interrelated activity. . . . Consequently, the rudimentary ecumenical organization which we saw in Columbus started out by fulfilling this primary purpose of community. The ecumenical organizations in Columbus which seemingly have succeeded are those which have moved to fulfill the emotional, the physical, the financial, and the intellectual needs of those who put a stake in the life of these small communities."[18] "It was evident in Columbus that one of the most pressing theological and ecclesiological issues has to do with community. . . . How can Christians of different traditions celebrate their oneness when they do experience it in ecumenical activities without violating the sacramental constraints of those traditions? In fact, with the current move toward openness and flexibility, it was evident in Columbus that pragmatic need is transcending historical formulations and traditions. Pragmatically the need for community seems to be transcending the ethnic and social sources of denominationalism and the resulting difference in practice."[19]

Dynamic worship in the unity we seek will result from the active participation of all God's people. A summary of the Columbus data regarding leadership and organizational style states: "All of this means that the styles by which organizations make their decisions, order their life and do their works are changing significantly. The representative principle is giving way to a participatory and negotiation style which requires the creative management of conflict. Interaction is being increased. Openness and flexibility are meant to facilitate and enable rather than to direct. Out of this common life, the community can authentically celebrate its oneness and its common purpose in creation."[20] "The shape of the unity we seek will be forged largely from the bottom-up."[21]

As for the integrity of Christian worship, the need for flexibility and diversity and for freedom of experimentation emerging from the Columbus data[22] supports the combination of freedom along with structure in the forms of worship. The close connection noted above between concern for the needs of others and ecumenical cooperation indicates that the worship we seek in unity will have an orientation to mission. Shared understanding of worship is an integral part of the "movement from the tolerance typical of denominationalism to the trust necessary for ecumenicity" which emerged from the Columbus data as a need for the unity we seek.[23]

* * * * *

Numerous recommendations are possible as a result of our study.[24] However, the totality of the data inclines us to recommend as of paramount importance an all-out effort to discover, disseminate, and win official approval of a creative solution to "what our consultation has found to be a neuralgic area—celebration of the Eucharist in common and reciprocal communion."[25] The object of this proposal is not a joint study of eucharistic doctrine, theology, and practice with a view to resolving all the conflicts in this area. The object is a solution to a critical impasse in ecumenical relations. It will involve theoretical principles but its aim is specific and pragmatic. An integral part of this search would be the project recommended by this consultation concerning belief as a source of unity and/or division. If the barriers around the Eucharist could be breached even to a limited extent, many lesser barriers around other elements of Christian worship would fall of themselves; on the other hand, overcoming these lesser barriers would not automatically bring down the barriers around the Eucharist because so much explicit and conflicting doctrine, theology, practice, and highly charged emotions have accumulated around this sacrament over the centuries.

We also recommend in a more pastoral vein that all the churches commit themselves to sponsoring a Year of Ecumenical Worship in 1980. Another year is possible, provided that it allows time for preparation. During this year the churches would cooperate in making known to one another and learning from one another the various heritages of Christian worship. They would explore the possibilities of worship in the unity we seek. Sermon and homily aids could be jointly prepared to assist preachers of all denominations on this theme. Agencies devoted to preparing religious instruction could be asked to develop the theme in their publications. Local congregations could invite nearby congregations of other denominations to join them in worship on Sunday. Roman Catholic bishops could encourage their people to fulfill their canonical Sunday obligation by responding to such invitations. In this year the churches in joint worship would celebrate Pentecost as a feast of the birth of the one Church. The Roman Catholic Federation of Diocesan Liturgical Commissions could be asked to take up this theme at its annual and regional conventions and to promote it in diocesan programs. The Liturgical Conference could be asked to stress the theme in its publications. Centers of liturgical studies could be asked to devote their programs to exploring the possibilities of worship together in the context of contemporary culture. During this year, jointly prepared and officially approved rites of baptism and marriage could be introduced for common use, especially in celebrations involving members of diverse denominations. Perhaps by this time some solution will have been found for the problem of eucharistic sharing.

This list of events for the Year of Ecumenical Worship is only illustrative. A joint commission appointed to manage the year's program would have as its first task imaginative planning for the year. Much could be learned from the experience of Key '73 as to what to do and what not to do for effectiveness.

Such a massive effort as this seems necessary to pull people out of their denominational preoccupations and raise the level of everyone's consciousness with regard to the problems, possibilities, and imperatives of worship together. More modest proposals will not break through institutional routine or capture the imagination.

Christopher Kiesling, O.P.

Notes

1. The forms reflecting traditions will be developments of the forms we now have. The new forms, while retaining continuity with the past, will involve notable discontinuity and thus be truly new. For various meanings of "reform" and their implications for worship, see Walter J. Burghardt, "Theologian's Challenge to Liturgy," *Theological Studies* 35 (1974):233-48.

2. The Pauline and Lucan accounts of institution imply a meal between the sharing of the bread and the partaking of the cup, while the Marcan and Matthean accounts imply that the two acts have been brought together (cf. 1 Cor. 11:25; Lk. 22:20; Mk. 14:23; Mt. 26:27).

3. Chapters 12-14 of 1 Corinthians are devoted to the problems occasioned by spontaneous prayer in the gatherings of the Corinthian church.

4. *Ministry in the Church: A Statement by the Theological Section of the Roman Catholic/Presbyterian-Reformed Consultation*, Richmond, Va., Oct. 30, 1971, no. 10.

5. *Ibid.*

6. *Reconsiderations: Roman Catholic / Presbyterian and Reformed Theological Conversations*, 1966-67, pp. 122-37, 139-53.

7. *Journal of Ecumenical Studies* 7 (1970):209-65. See also Franz Josef van Beeck, "Towards an Ecumenical Understanding of the Sacraments," *Journal of Ecumenical Studies* 3 (1966):57-112.

8. *Decree on Ecumenism*, no. 3, in Walter M. Abbott, ed., *The Documents of Vatican II* (New York: Guild Press, 1966), p. 346.

9. Secretariat for Promoting Christian Unity, *Directory 1967*, nos. 44-50.

10. See appendix.

11. Arleon L. Kelly, *Community and Institutional Factors in the Shape of the Unity We Seek: Sociological Input, Bi-Lateral Consultation, Columbus, Ohio*, no. 2.4.1, p. 11.

12. *Ibid.*, no. 2.4.2., p. 13.

13. *Ibid.*, nos. 2.2 and 2.3, pp. 9-11.

14. *Ibid.*, no. 5.1 (6), p. 25.

15. *Ibid.*, no. 2.4.1, pp. 12-13; see also *ibid.*, p. 13 on "denominationalism." For "need of fulfillment," see Eugene M. Burke, *Report on Presbyterian-Roman Catholic Task Force, Columbus, Ohio*, p. 3; and Sally Cunneen, *Report on Ecumenical Task Force Visit to Columbus, Ohio, Jan. 11-17, 1973*, p. 8.

16. *Ibid.*, no. 2.4.1, p. 12.

17. Burke, pp. 2-4, 9.

18. Kelley, no. 3.1.3, p. 21; see also Burke, pp. 3-4; Cunneen, pp. 6-8.

19. Kelley, no. 3.2, p. 21.

20. *Ibid.*, summary, p. 24.

21. *Ibid.*, no. 5.0, p. 24.

22. *Ibid.*, no. 5.1 (2) and (3), p. 24.

23. *Ibid.*, no. 5.1 (1), p. 24.

24. See Section D of the paper "Toward the Unity We Seek in Worship" in the appendix.

25. Burke, p. 3-4.